The Ethics of Care

In the series *Global Ethics and Politics*,
edited by CAROL GOULD

The Ethics of Care

A Feminist Approach to Human Security

Fiona Robinson

TEMPLE UNIVERSITY PRESS
Philadelphia

TEMPLE UNIVERSITY PRESS
Philadelphia, Pennsylvania 19122
www.temple.edu/tempress

Library of Congress Cataloging-in-Publication Data

Robinson, Fiona, 1965–
    The ethics of care : a feminist approach to human security / Fiona Robinson.
        p. cm. — (Global ethics and politics)
    Includes bibliographical references and index.
    ISBN 978-1-4399-0065-9 (cloth : alk. paper) —
    ISBN 978-1-4399-0066-6 (pbk. : alk. paper) —
    ISBN 978-1-4399-0067-3 (e-book)
    1. Caring—Moral and ethical aspects. 2. Feminist ethics. I. Title. II. Title:
Feminist approach to human security.
    BJ1475.R63 2011
    177'.7—dc22
                                                                            2011015102

Printed in the United States of America

121211-P

Contents

Acknowledgments

I am indebted to many people for their assistance and support in the writing of this book. Carol Gould, editor of the Global Ethics and Politics series, has been encouraging and helpful from the outset. Alex Holzman at Temple University Press has been an enthusiastic and supportive editor. Kim Hutchings, Josh Keton, and Carol Gould were generous with their time, reading and offering insightful comments on all or part of the manuscript. I am also grateful for the suggestions of four anonymous reviewers—two who read the initial proposal and two who read the completed manuscript.

I am fortunate to have had the opportunity to discuss the ideas in this book at a number of different conferences and colloquia over the past several years. I have watched and listened from the inside as the two the academic worlds that I inhabit—those of international relations and feminist philosophy—have begun to intersect in interesting and challenging ways. Conversations with Virginia Held, Alison Jaggar, Joan Tronto, and Christine Koggel have enriched my understanding of feminist ethics immensely.

My students have been a source of inspiration to me over the past fifteen years. During the writing of this book, I was lucky enough to work with three talented graduate students—Angela Livingstone,

Megan McIntosh, and Gabrielle Mason—whose research explored the importance of care ethics to diverse areas of political life. Angela and Gabrielle also served as superb research assistants as I wrote and prepared this book.

Of course, the day-to-day work involved in writing a book could not have occurred without the support and care of my family—my husband, Derek, and my children, Samuel and Olivia. This book is dedicated to them.

The Ethics of Care

Introduction

The future of social, emotional and caring work has tremendous implications for human well-being.

—FOLBRE AND NELSON 2000

Considering Care and Security

It is likely that most people consider "care" to be important—even fundamental—to their daily lives. Most families rely on relations of care—parents care for children, and often those same parents care for their own elderly parents. Family members care for one another when they are ill; for many who are fortunate, those illnesses are acute and not severe. For countless others, illness or disability is a day-to-day, relentless reality in which care must be constant and comprehensive.

Most people would also recognize the importance of care outside and beyond the nuclear and extended families. In most nation-states, some form of primary health care is available; certainly, the nature and quality of this care vary tremendously from state to state and are dependent upon a series of other economic, sociopolitical, and ideological factors. Other forms of care also exist in most states: child care and care for people who are disabled, chronically ill, or elderly. Much of this care is provided variously by the state—either centrally or at the provincial or municipal level—as well as by community organizations and private enterprises. In some cases, it is provided by migrant workers, who forfeit the opportunity to care for their own children in seeking the promise of paid "care work" in income-rich countries.

All social groups—from households to nation-states—must make decisions about how care will be organized. Human life as we know it would be inconceivable without relations of care. Despite the fundamental importance of care, many of us do not think much about it—who provides it or how and under what circumstances it is distributed. In many countries, such as Canada, where I currently reside and am a citizen by birth, many citizens have the luxury of not having to worry much about care. Although it may have many problems, Canada can still boast of one of the best health-care systems in the world. Living in an income-rich country, many Canadian families can provide, or purchase, care for their children and their elderly, disabled, or chronically ill family members. Despite the relatively high quality of care in Canada, a closer look at the situation of care even here raises a number of questions—questions about gender, race, and socioeconomic disparities. Many Canadians worry about the state of care in this country—not only our cherished health-care system but also the demand for child care in response to more and more women working outside the home, and the urgent need for elder care in the light of changing demographics. In Canada, as in all nation-states, poverty, race, and social exclusion cannot be disentangled from questions regarding the need for, and provision of, care.

In many other parts of the world, however, the situation in terms of care is much worse; for many people in developing countries, crises of care translate into immediate or long-term threats to human security. In sub-Saharan Africa, for example, the HIV/AIDS pandemic has created a crisis of care that is almost unimaginable. In Botswana and Zambia, an estimated 20 percent of children under the age of seventeen are orphans, with most orphaned as a result of HIV (UNAIDS 2008: 163). In India, the financial burden associated with HIV for the poorest households represents 82 percent of annual income (162). As the primary caregivers in Africa and other regions, women have seen their household and community burdens grow as a result of HIV, often compromising their health, their ability to generate income, and other markers of well-being (168).

In countries torn apart by years of military conflict, the adequate provision of care is a constant challenge. In areas of the world most affected by environmental change and degradation, adequate access to the natural resources required for daily life is difficult and sometimes impossible in the regions with the worst environmental disasters. As economic globalization continues, poor migrant women of color from low-income countries leave behind their own, often impoverished families to provide care work and other "intimate" labor abroad; it is this work that increasingly supports the affluent and globalized lifestyles of men and women in developed countries. When we consider care in this way, it becomes very difficult to argue that care is a "private" issue. Among the many aims of this book is to help confirm, perhaps in new ways, what feminist care ethicists have been arguing for over a decade: that the notion of care is a valuable political concept and that how we think about care is deeply implicated in existing structures of power and inequality (Tronto 1993: 21). I also seek to build on the idea that care is a *global* political issue and that decisions regarding the provision and distribution of care are of profound moral significance, insofar as they are central to the survival and security of people around the world.

But what does it mean to claim that care is a global issue? How could care possibly be related to international politics, much less to security? While states and institutions may not "care for" each other the way that individuals do, they must make decisions—including moral and financial decisions—about the distribution, nature, and quality of care for both their own citizens and, increasingly, those beyond their borders. As I argued in 1999, however, care is more than an "issue" in world politics; indeed, it can be understood as the basis for an alternative international political theory—one that challenges the instrumentalism of political realism, the normative ideas of liberalism, and the epistemology of rationalism that continue to shape our analytical lenses at the level of global politics (F. Robinson 1999).

My objective in this book, however, is to do more than simply advance an international political theory of care. This book aims to rethink security and, in particular, human security, through the lens of the ethics of care. It seeks to demonstrate, theoretically and through discussion of particular examples and contexts, why a thorough consideration of care in both ethical and practical terms is the best starting point if we are seeking to address the material, emotional, and psychological conditions that create insecurity for people. My goal is not to lay out a map or a utopian vision of how to achieve a more caring world; rather, it is to consider how our view of security in global politics would change once we recognize and accept not just interdependence among states but the ways responsibilities and practices of care grow out of relations of dependence and vulnerability among people in the context of complex webs of relations of responsibility. To this end, I explore the ways these relations are constructed by the interplay between discursive and representational practices of gender and race on the one hand, and the social relations of gender and production on the other. How we think about care—who is entitled to care and on what terms, who is responsible for care, how care is valued and remunerated—governs the decisions that are made regarding the nature of care at the household, community, state, and transnational levels.

This book is concerned with care both as a way of understanding ethics and as a set of practices. While the ethics of care has not yet entered the wider public consciousness in the way that the ethics of rights or the ethics of justice have, the term "care ethics" describes a now well-established and vibrant tradition of ethical thought that offers an alternative to the more mainstream traditions of rights and justice. Briefly, an ethics of care starts from a theory of the self as relational. In this view, the self has no "separate, essential core but, rather, becomes a 'self' through relations with others" (Hekman 1995: 73). Identity and subjectivity are thus not developed in isolation from other actors; rather, identities are mutually constituted. This understanding of subjectivity is tied to a specific social understanding of ontology. Relationality is thus a claim about the most basic nature of human social existence. Beyond the claim that humans are "social beings," the relational ontology of care ethics claims that relations of interdependence and dependence are a fundamental feature of our existence.

In addition to this relational ontology, an ethics of care regards morality as existing not in a series of universal rules or principles that can guide action but in the practices of care through which we fulfill our responsibilities to particular others. It argues that the nature and quality of relations of care are important and appropriate areas for moral inquiry. That these relations and the practices to which they give rise are most often directed toward particular others within relations of intimacy and proximity does not entail that the values and practices of care are of only "private" moral or social significance (and, by implication, of no political significance). On the contrary, relations of care and intimacy are of great political significance in that their form and nature are determined by relations of power that play out in a variety of different contexts—from the household to the global political economy.

My understanding of the ethics of care, however, parts company with the literature on care in which care is posited as normatively "good" and based on an unproblematic assumption of "need" (Cooper 2007: 244). As Kimberly Hutchings has argued, a feminist ethics of care is most powerful when voiced as a claim about the nature of the world we inhabit rather than a claim about what ought to be the case (2000: 123). That world is one in which moral reality is embedded in relations and practices of responsibility and recognition (123). This argument is in stark contrast to most justice-based moral reasoning, which asserts that morality is about the objective application of universalizable principles among mutually disinterested, disembodied individuals. By contrast, care ethicists claim that relationships matter morally; it is these relationships that give rise to responsibilities and practices of care. Relationships, however, do not simply arise naturally; they are constructed by material, discursive, and ideological conditions in a given context.

In this book I argue that relations of care in a global context are constructed by relations of power determined primarily by gender, class, and race. These are, in turn, structured by the discourses and materiality of neoliberal globalization and historical and contemporary relations of colonialism and neocolonialism. In this view, thinking about care in the context of global politics and security cannot posit a universal need for care as unproblematic or undifferentiated; needs are themselves constructed and produced by a wide range of relationships and structures. Care as a disposition is reflected in multiple and diverse relational contexts that shape needs and relations of power and define the nature of care. Relations of care are not always good or pure; indeed, part of the job of the care ethicist is to consider the conditions under which relations can, and often do, become relations of domination, oppression, injustice, inequality, or paternalism.

In addition to considering care ethics theoretically as the normative basis for rethinking human security, this book examines the more practical implications of relations of care for security in a variety of contexts: humanitarian intervention and peacebuilding, health, environment, and women's labor in the global economy. I argue that the responsibilities and labor associated with care can no longer be brushed aside as a "soft" or marginal issue; the provision of care and the distribution of care work are integral to the workings of the global political economy and to the human security of millions. As Saskia Sassen argues, the last decade has seen a growing presence of women in a variety of cross-border circuits that have become a source for livelihood, profit making, and the accrual of foreign currency (2002: 256). Sassen conceptualizes these developments as indicators of the "feminization of survival"; in other words, it is increasingly on the backs of low-wage and poor women that these forms of survival, profit making, and government revenue enhancement operate (274). Due in large measure to their growing role in the global political economy, relations of care are a central axis around which the security of all people, in the context of webs of relations, revolves. Assuming this is true, then the ways we think about, describe, and act in relation to care must be interrogated. In addition, we must consider the obstacles and inequities that currently serve to hinder the ability of many individuals and institutions (including states) to be attentive to care needs and that obstruct and prevent the equitable and adequate delivery of care in many contexts around the world.

It is probably already obvious that taking care seriously as the ethical and practical basis of human security will require a fairly dramatic rethinking of the nature of security and insecurity in the context of global politics. On the surface, the links between security and care may appear nonexistent; indeed, the two ideas may appear to be contradictory. As Jorge Nef argues, "security" is a multifaceted and often contradictory word (2008: 159). In the field of international relations, security is usually understood in military terms, insofar as militaries provide states with their security from external threats—in particular, other states. But militaries are not "caring" institutions; indeed, as Simon Dalby points out, they are primarily "designed, equipped and trained to break things and kill people" (2009: 4), not to nurture, listen, and respond with patience and attentiveness. This understanding of security implies the use of force, "legitimated" violence, and the exercise of sovereignty (Nef 2008: 159). But the term "security" is also applied to health and food; these constructions, along with "social security," are closely associated with second- and third-generation human rights, human development, and the maintenance of sustainable communities and livelihoods (159). Thus, the "national" and "human/social" understandings of security express starkly contrasting conceptions of global relations, interfaces between state and civil society, and the role of the state (159).

The word "security" is derived from the Latin root *securus*, which means "without care." Care in this sense refers to concern, worry, fear, or anxiety; thus, to be secure is to be "carefree," or without anxiety. As Liz Elliot argues, the impression here is that security "frees the individual from care or concern about her or his own safety, presumably to self-actualize without fear" (2007: 194). Interestingly, the *Oxford English Dictionary* defines "secure" as "untroubled by danger or apprehension" and "safe against attack," but it also includes "reliable, certain not to fail or give way" and "in safe keeping." These definitions point to a paradox inherent in the idea of security.

While achieving a state of freedom from anxiety or worry, or being carefree, may appear desirable, a superficial understanding of security as a condition achieved by an individual actor may mask networks of social relations—providing ongoing support and attentiveness to needs—required to even approach such a condition. In other words, a feeling of security is most often the product of feeling attached and included—a feeling that others are "here" with you to provide support. Furthermore, to speak of security as a carefree existence that may ultimately be achieved and sustained bears no resemblance to the realities of most people's lives—lives that are always already heavy with concern not only for themselves but also for a range of particular others for whom they take responsibility.

The focus of this book is not on state or national security; thus, its approach does not resemble the approaches to "security studies" dominant for decades in the discipline of international relations, especially in the United States. Moreover, while it is more closely aligned to the so-called critical security studies movement that has flourished since the late 1980s in Europe and Canada, it departs significantly from many of those major schools of thought. This book does not involve detailed analyses of security practices as "techniques of government" or of state and media discourses of security (see Huysmans 2006). Nor does it take an emancipatory approach, which would focus on achieving individual security through the realization of individual human rights (see Booth 1991). Rather, the feminist orientation of this book is manifest in a commitment to the project of revealing the effects of both discursive representations and material structures of gender through the application of different ontological lenses. Revealing the importance of moral relations of care for the security of most people around the world necessarily involves attention to the apparently "powerless" in societies—those who are constructed as weak, vulnerable, and dependent. As Maria Stern points out, much of the critical security studies literature focuses on "discourses of danger written by state security elites," yet there is very little work in "marginalized" sites (2006: 182–183). Those who care for others, and those who are most in need of care, are among the world's most marginalized people. This book seeks to illustrate why and how their security matters for our understanding of world politics.

A feminist care ethics perspective on security is inherently critical insofar as it reveals relations of power that are normally hidden from view and provides a method of analyzing the ways that these relations are connected to people's security. In particular, it allows us not only to recognize why most individuals and groups of people are not simply "autonomous" (like affluent businessmen) or "vulnerable" (like women and children, especially women of color in income-poor countries) but also to see how "autonomy" and "vulnerability" are constructed through the co-constitution of social relations and dominant norms and discourses. The lens of care allows us to see types of subjects—relational subjects—and threats to their human security that are normally hidden from view: elderly grandmothers in sub-Saharan Africa struggling to shoulder the burden of care for their adult children suffering from AIDS and their grandchildren orphaned by this pandemic; migrant women of color working as nannies, maids, or sex workers and the children they leave behind; and mothers who tolerate physical abuse because they lack independent means of support for themselves and their children. We also see women struggling to rebuild households and communities, and the networks of relations and sources of livelihood that uphold them, in the aftermath of violent conflict or natural disasters around the world. These women are certainly vulnerable to neoliberal economic reforms and feminized cross-border circuits of globalization (see Sassen 2002). But they are also agents who are using their skills as caregivers to meet their responsibilities for the security of their families and, often, members of their wider communities. We see *women* so often when we look through the lens of care because women shoulder the majority of the world's care work burden, and their moral agency tends to be characterized by practices of care toward particular others. To make this claim is not to make a claim about women's essential nature but about the feminization of care in most societies around the world.

It should be made clear at the outset, however, that this is not a book about *women's* security. When we look through the lens of care, we also see many men who are shouldering heavy burdens of care and who live every day with insecurity for themselves and their families. But we also see men detached from caring responsibilities—responsibilities that have been "feminized" and degraded by gender norms in a variety of contexts. As I discuss in the next chapter, it is crucial that we consider the possible ways in which the feminization and degradation of caring relations and practices, and the isolation of men from these roles, contribute to the construction of hegemonic forms of masculinity that are associated with violence. Violence here is understood as a continuum that includes domestic violence in the household and political violence within and among states. While this book takes a broad view of security that encompasses more than just physical violence and military threats, it also argues that these threats are not distinct from but intimately related to other forms of insecurity that result from a lack of attention to care in societies.

I do not offer care ethics as a prescription for achieving human security, but I do argue that a redescription can bring to light the ways in which the dominant approaches may be failing to illuminate how insecurity is experienced for many of the world's people. My redescription is based on three key points. First, *the "human" in human security cannot be understood as an autonomous individual; the human subjects of security must be understood as beings-in-relation.*[1] This is tied to the second point: *efforts to enhance human security must recognize the importance of relations and networks of responsibility and care in determining people's everyday experiences of security and insecurity.* Relations of care occupy a position of centrality in people's moral lives, as well as in their day-to-day activities. When these relations of care are damaged or severed, security is threatened. A critical feminist lens focuses our attention on these relations and activities rather than obscures them. I seek to distinguish this argument from liberal internationalist approaches that promote the West's "responsibility to protect" the vulnerable peoples and countries of the Global South. Thus, my third point: *an approach to human security based on a feminist care ethics challenges assumptions about dependency and vulnerability in world politics by reading care discourses and practices through historical and contemporary relations of domination and exclusion.*

In seeking to avoid the danger of paternalism, my approach to care ethics confronts the traditional formulation of "victims" in the human security literature. It challenges the static conceptualization of certain individuals and groups as dependent or vulnerable—women and children, developing countries, the poor—on empirical grounds. As Chapter 3 illustrates, women's care work can be empowering, and women's strategies for coping with poverty and care deficits demonstrate their resilience and active resistance in the face of economic and social obstacles. Furthermore, recognition of the increasing dependence of the Global North on the states of the Global South for the provision of care work challenges conventional understandings of the Global South as "dependent" on the Global North (F. Robinson 2010). If we look historically

---

[1] The term "beings-in-relation" is very close to Carol Gould's "individuals-in-relations" (1978); my "relational ontology" is also close to Gould's "social ontology." In *Globalizing Democracy and Human Rights*, she writes: "We begin from the principle of justice as equal positive freedom, which . . . is the normative conception that goes along with such a social ontology of individuals-in-relations and constituted social groups" (2004: 122). Conceptually, I am indebted to these formulations, insofar as they understand the self as constituted in and through relations (120). However, my formulation focuses primarily on affective relations of responsibility and care that may include, but are by no means limited to, relations among family members and friends rather than those existing among members of social groups such as nations, and ethnic or religious groups. I am grateful to Carol Gould for bringing this to my attention.

at patterns of dependence and interdependence among actors in global politics, it becomes clear that these patterns are subject to flux and transformation over the long term. Conceptually, my approach challenges the notion that dependence and vulnerability are something detrimental and temporary that must be overcome. While the balance and direction of dependence may change over time, dependence is a regular feature of human existence that, for some individuals and groups, is inevitable and permanent. All human beings are dependent on some others at times throughout their lives. The challenge is to integrate these empirical and conceptual insights into our theorizations of international politics in ways that eschew paternalism.

These arguments rest on the claims that well-being for people is achieved and sustained through relations and activities of care and that, in the absence of these relations or where they are deficient or disrupted, well-being and security are threatened. These are partly empirical claims; in other words, they rely on the work of sociologists and economists that has documented both the centrality of practices of care to the livelihoods of households and the workings of the global political economy. This work has also addressed the enormous inequality—by gender and race—present in this kind labor, both paid and unpaid. This book aims not simply to reiterate these claims but to consider theoretically the moral and practical implications of these inequalities, particularly through consideration of how the everyday conditions of people's lives are discursively and normatively constructed through ideas about the nature and value of care as a set of values and practices and, importantly, as a type of work. Especially important will be how these ideas are constructed through understandings of gender, "women's work," and the family and how these understandings serve to filter out considerations of care from the idea of human security.

A key implication of this new understanding of human security is that individual human rights will no longer be an adequate normative or analytical basis for understanding human security. Of course, securing rights for individuals can never be regarded as irrelevant or unimportant. This is particularly the case for women and other historically disadvantaged groups, including racial and ethnic minorities. As the analysis in Chapter 6 demonstrates, basic human and legal rights are crucial in the context of HIV/AIDS and human security. But the moral and transformative power of rights is most intense when rights are understood as "relational" and located within the wider context of care (see Minow 1990; Nedelsky 1993). Dominant liberal understandings of rights can no longer serve as a sufficient guide for ethical or policy deliberations aimed at mitigating human insecurity. Rather, attention must be directed toward the implications of various developments—in areas such as poverty, conflict, health, and environment—on the quality, stability, endurance, and resourcing of networks of caring relations at a variety of different scales.

Undoubtedly, my choice to invoke the term "human security" in this study will be controversial. Put simply, human security is widely understood as seeking to safeguard the "vital core of human lives from critical pervasive threats while promoting long-term human flourishing" (Alkire 2003). This idea—which arose in the immediate post–Cold War climate of the early 1990s—has attracted a remarkable amount of attention, much of it critical. At a time when traditional security concerns seemed less relevant and attention was able to refocus on the "everyday" insecurities of poverty, human security provided a framework for considering the impact not of external threats for states but of long-term vulnerabilities for people. Of course, the human security paradigm has generated much criticism; it has been described as "hot air" (Paris 2001), "reductionist" and idealistic" (Buzan 2004), and "inscrutable" (Paris 2004). In a comprehensive list, Ken Booth describes the range of critiques that have been articulated against human security: analytically, it is regarded as vague, unwieldy, and too expansive; in terms of policy, it has been criticized as being impossible to measure, giving a false sense of priorities, deflecting attention away from war, and simply reformulating existing human rights measures (2007: 322–323). Much critique has been focused on human security as a "paradigm," as a discourse, and as a foreign policy strategy of governments, especially the Canadian government. As Edward Newman points out, the policy orientation of human security—and its adoption as a policy framework by some governments—has made scholars of critical security studies suspicious of human security as a hegemonic discourse co-opted by the state (2010: 77). More recently, it is widely thought that human security's day is done—that the space for considering security in this way has now disappeared, especially in the light of recent geopolitical and economic developments.

Perhaps the most damning critique is that human security potentially reinforces the unequal nature of the contemporary global order by unintentionally legitimizing two of the principal features of the post-9/11 world order: "democratic imperialism"—the result of liberal internationalism—and neoliberal or "predatory" globalization (Shani 2007: 18–19). Closely related is the claim that "human security" as a discursive concept functions to securitize realms of human life—biological and bare life—not previously subject to security's purview and control and functions as a form of biopolitics (Berman 2007: 31). Thus, human security discourse simultaneously repeats national security's structuring logic and extends/empowers it to take control of "bare life" as such (31; see also Duffield 2002).

I am sympathetic to these critiques; indeed, I am well aware of the potential for human security discourses to become a technique of governmentality or a project of paternalism. As I discuss in Chapter 5, paternalism is a particular danger of care ethics that must be addressed. It should be made very clear that my aim is *not* to replicate the politics of those critical and human security approaches that revolve around the concept of emancipation, where the agent of emancipation is almost invariably the West (Barkawi and Laffey 2006: 350). I do maintain that the idea of human security still has relevance—and may indeed have renewed importance—in spite of the changes in security politics since 2001. While attention and resources have, in the last near decade, been drawn to the "war on terror" and other "new security threats"—drugs, organized crime, "human" trafficking—they have simultaneously been drained from the ongoing, often deepening crises of poverty and health, especially in the Global South. Furthermore, at the time of writing, the world is in the midst of a major global economic downturn that is refocusing attention and opening up space for discursive shifts and policy innovations. While the focus of attention tends to be on the hit taken by large Western economies, especially that of the United States, the crises in many countries of the Global South continue to deepen.

Despite the association of human security approaches with largely uncritical and theoretically unsophisticated, policy-relevant, Western-centric literature, there exists within the idea of human security the potential to develop an approach to security studies that foregrounds the insecurities of people in the context of their real lives in ways that do not reproduce familiar dichotomies between the powerful and the powerless, North and South, protectors and protected. Furthermore, while a care ethics approach to human security is neither an emancipatory theory nor an explicitly policy-relevant approach to security, it is committed to the possibility of progressive change in the day-to-day lives of all people. While it is important, as Booth argues, to recognize the extent to which the (state) practices associated so far with the concept of human security work to maintain the status quo, it is also important to consider the fundamental changes in attitudes and behavior of governments that are required in order to begin to overcome "systemic human insecurity" (2007: 326).

By foregrounding and prioritizing the consideration of the politics of care, we can recover the potential of human security to focus attention on innovative strategies for addressing exclusion and oppression that are neither Western-centric nor imperialistic. This approach would critique, rather than reempower, the institutions and processes of neoliberal globalization and would recognize the need to distribute responsibilities for well-being in ways that are democratic and equitable. Considering security through the lens of care need lead neither to depoliticization nor to a focus on "bare life"; on the contrary, it may lead us to a greater awareness of the complexity of care in the contemporary world and the spatially extensive and diverse matrix of social relations and political deliberations on which it relies.

It is widely understood that human security approaches understand security "comprehensively and holistically in terms of the real-life, everyday experiences of human beings" and shift the focus of security studies from the "security dilemma of states" to the "survival dilemma of people" (Hudson 2005: 163). As I discuss in Chapter 2, feminists have cautiously embraced the idea of human security, welcoming the broadening of security beyond its conventional military focus and state-centrism while critiquing the ungendered human subject of security. Despite these feminist interventions, there is little work that addresses human security from the perspective of care ethics and care work. One notable exception is the work included in the edited collection *Engendering Human Security: Feminist Perspectives* (Truong, Wieringa, and Chhachhi 2006). The editors of this collection argue convincingly that there remains something inherently important about an approach to security that advocates a redirection of policy concerns from a state-based to society-based framework and intends to emphasize the significance of quotidian needs and conditions of common people. They note, moreover, that virtually all approaches to human security have failed to recognize the extent to which care as "maintenance" is a foundation of the human condition that makes the "continuity of life and social institutions possible" (xviii–xix). I seek to build on these important observations through philosophical analysis and through illustrations of the importance of care in a number of contexts in global politics.

Notes on Methodology

As described previously, the purpose of this book is to reconsider human security theoretically through the lens of a feminist ethics of care. It is not primarily a work of security studies. Indeed, the trajectory of my research to date has always been, and continues to be, driven by inquiry into effects of using different ethical lenses in circumscribing and enabling various aspects of world politics. Moreover, I have long been interested specifically in the implications of looking at politics through *feminist* ethical lenses, since these are widely seen by moral theorists to be irrelevant to ethics and by international political theorists to be irrelevant to public, and certainly to global political, life. Thus, while my approach is, broadly speaking, that of normative international relations theory (IR theory), I do not seek to develop a definitive, universal "ethics" of security. Rather, as I have discussed elsewhere, I see the business of "doing" ethics in IR as, primarily, a critical activity (see F. Robinson 2006c). Thus, in undertaking this activity, my job is not to prescribe a set of norms or moral principles upon which a theory of global justice, for example, or a theory of global ethics can be constructed. Rather, in this approach, the role of the normative theorist is to interrogate critically the ethical ideas that prevail in given contexts and to consider the political implications of those ethics. Political philosophy, including international political philosophy, is in this sense a critical activity, as James Tully has so clearly described:

> It seeks to characterize the conditions of possibility of the problematic form of governance in a redescription (often in a new

vocabulary) that transforms the self-understanding of those subject to and struggling within it, enabling them to see its contingent conditions and the possibilities of governing themselves differently. Hence, it is not only an interpretive political philosophy but also a specific genre of critique or critical attitude toward ways of being governed in the present—an attitude of testing and possible transformation. (2002: 534)

It is, again in Tully's words, a species of "practical philosophy" (politics and ethics), that is, a philosophical way of life oriented toward working on ourselves by working on the practices and problematizations in which we find ourselves (534). This task necessarily entails a descriptive and empirical burden—indeed, one that is far greater than is commonly thought (M. Walker 1998: 13). While it does not involve an ethnographically thick description that aims at clarification or understanding for its own sake (Tully 2002: 534), critical moral inquiry bears a distinctive moral and political responsibility to "seek out and entertain many distinct moral understandings that supply a going social-moral order" (M. Walker 1998: 13–14). It is, in this sense, "political philosophy for Earthlings," as David Miller puts it in his 2008 essay of the same title. Understood in this way, political philosophers "must also be social scientists, or at least be prepared to learn from social scientists." They must consider what it would mean to implement the principles they prescribe and discover whether the "ensuing consequences are acceptable, in the light of the fundamental beliefs of their fellow citizens" (Miller 2008: 47).

Feminists, by and large, have always been especially good at ensuring that their political philosophy was "for Earthlings"; in other words, a hallmark of feminist research has been situated, contextual analysis that takes as its starting point the concrete realities of women's daily lives. Indeed, some feminists have insisted on drawing a sharp dichotomy between abstract concepts and concrete reality in order to argue that the "reality of women's lives" constitutes a given reality that provides a necessary grounding for feminist theory. In contrast, I would argue, with Susan Hekman, that "women's reality" is itself a socially constructed discursive formation constituted by shared concepts (Hekman 1997: 361). But this does not render it politically meaningless;

recognizing the ways realities are discursively constructed discounts neither the social origins of those discourses nor their impact on real people's lives. As Hekman argues, the fact that women's reality is "closely tied to the social actors' own concepts and provides a counter to the hegemonic discourse of masculinist science makes it no less a discourse" (355). Hekman articulates this point clearly in the case of feminist standpoint theory: "Feminist standpoint theory can and, I argue, should be defined as a counterhegemonic discourse that works to destabilize hegemonic discourse. But this can be achieved without denying that it is a discourse or according it epistemological privilege" (355). In this sense, feminism constitutes an important feature of the theoretical methodology employed in this book and of my version of the ethics of care. I agree with the claim made by Nancy Hartsock that feminism is, at bottom, a mode of analysis—a method of approaching life and politics rather than a set of political conclusions about the oppression of women (1981: 35). Again, however, it should be emphasized that this does not render feminism politically neutral or disabled; on the contrary, from this perspective, the values and the interests of the investigator are integral to the way in which the research is undertaken. Thus, the aim is not to uncover a new or more complete or better "truth" but to "create a set of ideal types that allow us to 'see' a different world" (Hekman 1997: 361).

Chapter Overview

Chapter 1 explores the ethics and practices of care and places both in the context of existing literatures. In the first part of the chapter, I outline in detail my understanding of the nature and scope of a feminist ethics of care. The second part focuses specifically on the relationship between care, masculinities, and violence. This understanding of ethics provides both the theoretical framework and the methodological approach for my analysis of the ethics of human security.

Chapter 2 addresses the idea of security in world politics. It focuses primarily on critical, human, and feminist security studies. I argue that a care ethics approach to human security draws on all three of these broad schools of thought but that there are important differences that distinguish it; the result is a complete rethinking of the most basic idea of security and what might be necessary in efforts to work toward achieving it.

Chapter 3 grounds these arguments by placing them in the context of contemporary global social relations of care. By focusing on "women's work" in the global care and sex economies, this chapter reveals the ways in which changes in social relations—including the intensified transnationalization and commodification of care—create new challenges of security connected to care. Contemporary feminist analysis requires that unequal relations within a household have to be situated within an international division of reproductive labor that is structured by social class, "'race'/ethnicity as well as gender inequalities" (Yeates 2005: 232). I consider these flows in relation to the wider movement of poor women across borders for sex, domestic, and other low-wage labor.

Chapter 4 explores the relationship between the social relations and discourses of care on the one hand and the dominant normative understandings of "global security governance" on the other. One aim of this chapter is to consider how we might rethink the ethics and politics of humanitarian intervention when looking through the lens of care ethics. I argue that the relational ontology of a critical feminist ethics of care—which emphasizes human interdependence and mutual vulnerability—overcomes the dichotomies between the needy and the strong, victims and agents, and objects and subjects in the construction of categories in humanitarian intervention. Combined with the revised view of human security outlined in earlier chapters, this approach also destabilizes the inside-outside dichotomy by pushing theorists and policy makers to look at the state of care within their own societies. Finally, it breaks down the distinction between crisis and normality, putting the very idea of humanitarian intervention in question. If we were to look through the lens of care ethics, then greater attention would be focused on the permanent background to identified "humanitarian crises" in order to better understand how gender relations, as well as those based on religion, ethnicity "culture," race, and class, affect the real, day-to-day lives and security of people, their families, and their communities. A narrative, rather than a principled approach to moral judgment, would demand attention be paid to the particularities of different humanitarian emergencies, including the relationship between the situations and wider social, economic, and geopolitical relations and processes.

Chapter 5 explores the "rebuilding" aspects of human security through the lens of care ethics. It is widely recognized that peacebuilding is a crucial aspect of human security; however, the dominance of the so-called liberal peace either ignores considerations of care or gives rise to paternalistic care. This chapter addresses theoretically the dangers of paternalism in care ethics and argues for the importance of reading care through neocolonialism in the context of peacebuilding.

Chapter 6 explores human security implications of health, focusing on HIV/AIDS in sub-Saharan Africa, through the lens of a critical, feminist ethics of care. The first section in the chapter concentrates primarily on the material conditions and impact of the care crisis; the second blends material and discursive analysis to provide an analysis of the link between hegemonic masculinities and forms of HIV/AIDS-related violence. Specifically, this section examines violence against women, which includes violence in the home and militarized sexual violence, in relation to HIV/AIDS. Addressing gender-based violence in terms of hegemonic masculinities and the feminization of care can shed light on the significance of gender relations in transforming cultures of violence and enhancing security for women, men, and children who are living with the realities of AIDS.

Chapter 7 explores the ethics of global environmental security. I argue that, examined through the lens of care ethics, the health and flourishing of the natural environment must be seen as inextricably connected to our ability to give and receive the care necessary for basic human security. While there is much debate in the literature regarding whether or not care ethics is strategically or conceptually appropriate as a lens through which to consider the relationship of human beings (and often, specifically, women) to the environment, I argue that this arises when care is understood in highly essentialist, apolitical terms. When care ethics is politicized—through interrogation of the global political economy of care as part of a feminist political agenda seeking just and sustainable societies—these "dangers" are mitigated.

1 | The Ethics of Care and Global Politics

W hile the concept of care still remains on the margins of academic analyses of social, moral, and political life, the past two decades have witnessed a remarkable growth in this field of study. Research from moral and political philosophy into the ethics of care continues to develop, and while recent books employ a diversity of approaches, they all contribute to consolidating its place as a serious and important alternative to dominant Kantian and rights-based ethics (Held 2006; Engster 2007; Slote 2007). In addition, there has been a recent proliferation of analyses of the role and nature of care work in domestic, comparative, and global contexts. Feminist economists and sociologists have convincingly shown how and why unpaid or underpaid care work—performed largely by women—demands a rethinking of traditional theories of economics, global political economy, and globalization (Peterson 2003; Beneria 2003, 2008). This research includes work related to care and domestic/global social policy, migrant domestic workers, and "global care chains" and has contributed to theoretical/conceptual debates about the nature of economic globalization (Sevenhuijsen 1998; Parreñas 2001; Ehrenreich and Hochschild 2002).

Moreover, scholars are increasingly making an effort to integrate the moral philosophy of care ethics with analyses of care work and social policy. Fiona Williams (2001) relies on her empirical sociological research on Britain and Western Europe to advance a new political ethics of care. Olena Hankivsky (2004) uses the ethics of care to ground her analysis of Canadian social policy in the fields of health, law, and economics. Moreover, a number of moral philosophers addressing the ethics of care have effectively integrated care ethics with "real-world" social and political problems (Held 2006; Gould 2004). A recent edited volume on the ethics and social politics of care seeks to integrate the ideas and literatures on the ethics and social politics of care from a transnational perspective (Mahon and Robinson, forthcoming).

Not surprisingly, there is a clear emphasis on care as an economic issue in much of this literature. Recognizing care as a kind of "work" has important implications for our understandings of labor, value, globalization, and even the economy itself. It also has massive transformative implications in that it challenges gender roles, long-standing assumptions about the role of social policy and the "welfare state," and contemporary ideological and policy perspectives on globalization. As such, this economic analysis of care is to be welcomed, especially by feminists seeking to address women's relative power and well-being but also by all those who question the contemporary neoliberal emphasis on individual self-sufficiency and economic growth.

In this book, I seek to build out from these important literatures in order to broaden the relevance of care beyond the realms of economics, social policy, and economic globalization to the arena of security. This interest in care and security arose initially from my hypothesis that both the dominant discourses of care and the contemporary global distribution of care work and services are constitutive of and reproduced through not only recent developments in global capitalism but also norms and discourses related to masculinity and femininity. In this view, the material and discursive processes that link care to femininity—increasingly a racialized femininity—simultaneously construct a dichotomous logic whereby dominant or "hegemonic" masculinities are characterized by a disassociation with the values and practices of care. Familiar feminine constructions of embodiment, emotion, and dependence are set against hegemonic masculine characteristics associated with rationality, autonomy, and certain forms of militarized, state-sanctioned violence.

While certain types of violence are gendered masculine and associated with conventional security studies, feminists have taught us that violence must be understood as a continuum that includes both intimate violence and militarized violence sanctioned by states and international organizations (see Cockburn 2004). Understood in this way, violence cannot be separated into distinct categories of "private" and "public"; rather, various manifestations of violence are often overlapping and may be traced to similar normative and discursive roots.

A wealth of research is devoted to elucidating the connections between hegemonic forms of masculinity, militaries and militarism, and violence. Theorists have shown convincingly, for example, how gendered discourses and imagery are used in the "making" of soldiers (see Cohn 1987). Feminists have also written much on the ways and extent to which gender essentialisms—which associate women with nurturing—have served to reify their roles as carers, thus erecting normative and structural obstacles to their full participation in "public life." But there has been relatively little inquiry into the relationship between masculinities, care, and violence. In this book I argue, in contrast, that a full understanding of human insecurity—not only for women but for all people—must address this relationship. For example, what happens to societies in which care work is seen to be appropriate only for marginalized groups—especially poor migrant women of color? While feminists have begun to address the important implications of this trend for the migrant women themselves, there may be other, wider effects in societies, such as the strengthening of hegemonic forms of masculinity, including violent masculinities, the deepening of men's exclusion from caring activities, and the general devaluing of care as a priority at the level of national and global social policy. All of these effects have, in turn, important implications for the security of women, men, and children.

This chapter outlines the development of care ethics through reference to the literature in ethics and political theory and sets out the particular approach to care ethics taken in this book. The discussion builds on the understanding of care ethics developed in *Globalizing Care* (F. Robinson 1999); however, this version addresses the importance of considering norms and representations of masculinity and femininity in examining both the ethics and practices of care in relation to human security. I argue that these norms and representations—particularly in their dominant or hegemonic form—are traceable, in some important respects, to different understandings of the nature of care and caregiving in different social contexts. Finally, I suggest that devaluing the activities of care may contribute to the maintenance of "cultures of violence" in various contexts, from the family to the transnational level.

The Ethics of Care

The ethics of care—while still relatively unknown in the discipline of international relations—now boasts a well-developed literature in the fields of feminist moral, political, and legal theory, as well as in sociology and social policy. Informed by the early work of Carol Gilligan (1982), Sara Ruddick (1980, 1989), and Nel Noddings (1986), the ethics of care has been developed by moral and political philosophers and legal and social theorists. While the earliest work on care ethics concentrated on care as an alternative to justice as a form of moral reasoning, later works sought to interrogate the political implications of care (Tronto 1993; Sevenhuijsen 1998). Indeed, it may be more correct to say that many feminist scholars—in philosophy, political theory, and legal studies—took seriously the powerful political implications of Carol Gilligan's early findings regarding gendered differences in responses to a variety of moral dilemmas. While a significant number of feminist scholars were wary—of essentialism, of the reification of stereotypes, or of glossing over differences among women—a large group of feminists from a variety of disciplines have recognized the enormous significance of bringing care, as an approach to understanding morality and as a type of work, out of the private sphere. In so doing, these feminists are seeking not to transfer care from homes to states but rather to deconstruct the gendered dichotomies that have created the public and private spheres as two separate realms of human existence.

More recently, research on care ethics and care work has begun to explore care in a global context (F. Robinson 1999, 2006a, 2006b, 2008; Hutchings 2000; Held 2006; Porter 2007; Lawson 2007; Hankivsky 2006; Kittay 2005). In 2006, Elizabeth Porter argued that there has been minimal application of the themes of care ethics to political issues in international relations, where the care of distant humans is paramount (99).[1] Her article, and her 2007 book, elaborate on what she calls a "politics of care" and a "politics of compassion" in the context of international peacekeeping; she describes these normative under-standings of politics as linking the universal and the particular in that they assume "a shared humanity of interconnected, vulnerable people and [require] emotions and practical, particular responses to different expressions of vulnerability" (2006: 99; 2007). In her 2006 book, *The Ethics of Care: Personal, Political and Global*, Virginia Held suggests that the ethics of care is "beginning to influence how those interested in international relations and global politics see the world and our respon-sibilities in it, and it holds promise for new efforts to improve global relations" (155). Like Porter, she argues that a global ethics of care can be constructed in order to extend caring moral responses beyond the realm of private or personal relationships to the global context.

While accounts of the nature of the ethics of care differ, it is pos-sible to isolate a number of key attributes of the "substance" of care ethics that distinguish it from other approaches to ethics. In a succinct and clear statement, Virginia Held argues that the ethics of care focuses on the "compelling moral salience of attending to and meeting the needs of particular others for whom we take responsibility" (2006: 10). Joan Tronto's now well-known formulation highlights the importance in care ethics not of moral principles as such but of *practices* as con-stitutive of morality. These include attentiveness, responsibility, nur-turance, compassion, and meeting others' needs (1993: 3). But while there is widespread agreement among feminist ethicists and political philosophers regarding the substantive characteristics of care ethics—the relational ontology and the substantive features of ethics that flow from that—there is rather less agreement regarding epistemological and methodological questions in care ethics. Care ethicists—and feminist moral philosophers more broadly—have differing views on epistemol-ogy and, specifically, the nature and status of moral judgment in the ethics of care, the "form" of care ethics (as opposed to traditional moral theories), and the methods of moral inquiry that arise from a feminist ethics of care.

---

[1] Porter cites F. Robinson 1999 as a "notable exception" to this. Other examples include the works cited previously.

My own approach to these issues is informed by the work of Margaret Walker and Kimberly Hutchings, who both devote considerable intellectual energy to questions of epistemology and methodology in feminist ethics. For both Walker and Hutchings, feminist ethics involves two tasks of equal importance: "reflective analysis" and "critical reflection" (M. Walker 1998: 11). Because, for both of these thinkers, morality is neither "pure" nor separate from social life, the first task of morality is to really look at moral arrangements in particular contexts and consider how they "inhere in and are reproduced by interactions between people, and how moral orders are concretely embodied in social ones" (M. Walker 1998: 11). For this, the moral philosopher may rely on many kinds of research, including, as I do in this book, research done by sociologists and economists on the transnationalization of care work.

The second task of moral philosophy, according to Walker, is "critical reflection on features and conditions of specific forms of moral life" (1998: 11). This kind of reflection asks whether the nature of existing moral orders makes the "right kinds of sense" to all of the participants; in so doing, it is ultimately concerned with the "discourses, procedures and relations of authority that make it possible for some understandings to prevail" (60). For feminists, in particular, this critical attention is attuned to the implications of particular moral orders for gender relations, as well as other intersecting power relations, including those related to race and class.

These two tasks that Walker describes correspond loosely to what Hutchings has called the "phenomenological" and "genealogical" tasks of ethics. The first involves recognizing, or indeed putting into place, the conditions within which moral arguments will be intelligible. This task flows from the recognition that "moral judgments make sense within contexts" (Hutchings 2000: 122). The genealogical element of feminist ethics, moreover, involves investigation of the role of gender in the establishment of particular moral judgments as expressions of "ethical necessity," as well as in the construction and maintenance of particular patterns of benefits and costs associated with those judgments (122).

For both Walker and Hutchings, feminist ethics has tremendous critical capacity. Walker's idea of "moral understandings" comprises a collection of "perceptive, imaginative, appreciative and expressive skills and capacities which put and keep us in unimpeded contact with the realities of ourselves and specific others" (M. Walker 1989: 21). Embedded in this way of thinking about ethics, she argues, are a number of "potent critical resources" (21). These are of great significance to the construction of a critical feminist ethics of world politics:

> The obvious ones I see are its structural capacity to challenge "principled" moral stances in the concrete, where these are surrogates for or defenses against, responsiveness in actual relationships; to export an insistence on the primacy of personal acknowledgement and communication to institutional and "stranger" contexts; and on a philosophical plane to pierce through the rhetoric of ethics to the politics of ethics as a routine matter. (146)

Eschewing epistemological foundationalism and moral universalism, Walker defends an epistemology that she defines as "naturalized" *and* "critical." While this epistemology is not *fully normative* in the strong sense, it still retains normativity. In other words, it does not attempt to see whether a particular way to live is indeed "how to live" for human beings as such; however, it does hold particular moral understandings to some standards of shared intelligibility, and it asks whether they are better or worse than some other ways we might know or imagine (M. Walker 1998: 12–13).

Finally, in contrast to traditional rights-based or Kantian moral theory, this approach to feminist ethics relies on a narrative structure of moral understanding. Rather than apply principles to cases, narrative structure rests on the idea that a story is the basic form of representation of moral problems (M. Walker 1998: 68). Narrative structure requires knowledge of the "characters," their relationships, their histories, and their identities. This approach does not imply a descent into moral relativism; rather, it implies a recognition that situations in which moral contexts are not shared should not be seen as inevitably leading to conflict but as opportunities to disrupt, challenge, and redescribe the social contexts in which moral discourse emerges and thus to reveal the possibility of common ground or shared meanings and even to begin to put in place the conditions under which these may emerge.

Following the epistemological and methodological insights of feminist ethicists like Walker and Hutchings, my approach to care ethics is a *critical theory*. The ethics of care becomes critical, I argue, when it is committed to looking at "where moral views are socially sited and what relations of authority and power hold them in place" (M. Walker 1998: 75). The critical lens of care ethics exposes the ways in which dominant norms and discourses sustain existing power relations that lead to inequalities in the way societies determine how and on what bases care will be given and received. In this way, it distances itself from what Cooper calls "normative" or "idealized" care scholarship (2007: 253). While early feminist scholarship on the ethics of care provided a solid basis for critiquing traditional moral philosophy and rethinking the substance of morality, its tendency to idealize caring relationships and posit care as morally superior to justice ethics is troubling and problematic.

By contrast, my approach to care ethics is primarily concerned with making an ontological claim—as Hutchings writes, "a claim about the nature of the world we inhabit rather than a claim about what ought to be the case" (2000: 123). I argue, however, that in making that ontological shift—one that allows us to see moral subjects as relational and to recognize ethics as fulfilling responsibilities through practices of care— we reveal new possibilities for how to ensure that those responsibilities can be fulfilled in a manner that minimizes exclusion and suffering.[2] Hence, claims about what ought to be the case are never abandoned entirely. But these claims cannot be judged or justified according to some transcendent or external standpoint—rather, they are always context dependent and always subject to revision and reconfirmation. As Selma Sevenhuijsen argues, the moral agent in an ethics of care stands "with both feet in the real world"; this is in contrast to the ideal moral agent of universalist ethics, which must abstract from specific circumstances in order to achieve responsible moral judgment. But, she argues, situatedness in concrete social practices need not be seen as a threat to

---

[2] Carol Gould makes a similar argument about the relationship between ontological and normative claims. She argues that her "social ontology" is itself already in a way normative—that the very characterization of individuals as agents or persons with cultural identities supports an argument for certain rights as valid claims of such individuals (2004: 121).

independent judgment; indeed, the ethics of care demands reflection on the best course of action in specific circumstances (1998: 59).

Having presented the epistemological and methodological assumptions that provide the groundwork for thinking about morality in this way, I return briefly to the key ontological and substantive aspect of relationality and contextuality. To reiterate, an ethics of care must include the following: First, it requires a relational ontology. As I discuss in the Introduction, while this is an argument about the nature of the self as existing in relation to others, it is necessarily tied to an ontological account of how human subjects lead their lives. Second, care ethics involves a focus on attention, responsiveness, and responsibility to the needs of particular others as the substance of morality. Third, it demands a commitment to addressing moral problems in the historical and spatial contexts of real, lived experiences. Finally, the ethics of care involves a reconceptualization of traditional understandings of the nature of and relationship between the public and private spheres.

The first feature of care ethics—the relational ontology—is the philosophical starting point of this approach and the point from which all its other claims about morality and human flourishing flow. Because it is informed by the claim that human life is sustained through care, the ethics of care relies on two related arguments about ontology: (1) that the self is properly understood as relational, and thus morality can be said to exist only in the context of the self in relation with others, and (2) what Hutchings calls a "a higher-level ontological assumption" that relationships of care and responsibility are the key to understanding "moral substance" as such (2000: 123). These ontological claims depart radically from the individualistic, justice-based approaches that dominate not only moral and political philosophy but also IR theory.

The dominant ontology of autonomy—of isolated, self-reliant moral selves—does not adequately reflect people's lived experience in most communities around the world. Feminist moral and political philosophers have argued that one of the effects of this ontology has been to obscure from view the particular experiences of women, who are most likely to define themselves in and through their relationships with children and other family members—including those who are elderly or chronically ill—or with friends or members of their communities. This is not to say, however, that the picture of "autonomous man" only distorts the experiences of women; indeed, care ethicists argue that all people—both women *and* men—live lives that are, at least during some periods of time, interdependent with those of others and that moral analysis must reflect, rather than obscure, this fundamental characteristic of human existence.

While the need for care is universal, a feminist ethics of care is not a universalistic ethics in the traditional sense. It is an ethics of particularism in that it rejects the claim that the highest stage of moral learning is characterized by disinterest and noninterference (Gilligan 1993: 18). In contrast to a reflective understanding of human rights, in which the individual is primary, the ethics of care is based on a morality of responsibility in which the emphasis is on connection, and the relationship itself, rather than the individuals in it, is primary (19). Moreover, it is also necessary to pay attention to the particular situational contexts in which people are immersed that may render their need for care different, or more or less acute. As Eva Kittay has argued, there appear to be universal aspects of meaning and experience of caring, including, at a most basic level, that it is required by all human beings at some time in their lives. However, differences in ability, race, gender, sexuality, religion, culture, and geography orient us differently toward care; it is this *construction of care*, then, that makes questions concerning the giving and receiving of care a matter of social, moral, and political import (Kittay 2005: 444–445).

The particularism and contextualism of care ethics are among its most controversial features. This can be explained in two ways: The first source of hostility to this view of ethics arises from the dominance of traditional approaches to ethics that call for impartiality and universality in moral thinking and that rely on the application of abstract rules to particular moral situations. Morality is said to demand that the moral agent be able to remove himself or herself from the emotional, private feelings that are seen to characterize our responses in the context of personal relationships; indeed, the highest stage of morality is seen to be characterized by a morality of rationality that can apply moral principles without bias. As Tronto argues, this kind of approach to ethics presumes that we think most clearly about others when we think of them as distant from us (1993: 13). "Closeness" is seen to lead to "clouded" moral thinking and, ultimately, to partiality, favoritism, and nepotism.

This argument, however, relies on a caricature of care ethics as counseling that moral attention should be bestowed on those "near and dear" or, worse, those who are in some ways "like" us. No version of care ethics that I have come across argues this. Rather, care ethicists argue that people experience their moral lives in the context of webs of relationships with individuals and groups of particular others and that one of the main tasks of moral inquiry is to think about how care and responsibilities for care are distributed both within and across societies. This does not preclude concern for distant others or those who are not like us; on the contrary, this approach actually offers us resources for critical evaluation of the nature of responsibilities of care leading to revisions in resolutions of important questions regarding the distribution, resourcing, and recognition of our moral responsibilities to others.

The second source of hostility toward the particularism of care ethics comes from the frequent invocation of the mother-child relationship as paradigmatic of this approach to morality. This has been wrongly interpreted as suggesting that there is a natural or essential link between women's identity and motherhood or as idealizing the mother-child relationship as morally superior and thus ignoring the conflict, power imbalances, indifference, and even cruelty that can potentially characterize it. This reading ignores the fact that those who use this example do so in order to provide a *model* of moral reasoning from which important moral values can be derived (see Held 1993). However, there may be other problems with relying too heavily on the mother-child model; as Selma Sevenhuijsen argues, associating the "mother figure" with values such as concreteness, care, and compassion as opposed to abstraction and justice runs the risk of reproducing the mode of arguing in binary oppositions with which Western thinking is so thoroughly permeated (1998: 13). Moreover, this model may serve to direct attention away from the political aspects of care and the more basic questions of the quality of moral identities and moral subject positions that feminists construct in their reasoning (13).

Following theorists such as Joan Tronto, my vision of the ethics of care is committed to a radical reconceptualization of the public-private dichotomy—especially as it has developed in Western societies and "international society" through the legacy of Western liberalism. This means, most obviously, a rethinking of the nature of the "moral boundaries" of public and private as they relate to ethics and politics (Tronto, 1993). In particular, it must challenge the assertion in most moral and political philosophy that care matters in the context of intimate, personal relationships but that it is irrelevant, or dangerous, in the real context of ethics—the public realm. But challenging this account of public and private ethics must be part of a wider contestation of what counts as political and how these assumptions are fundamentally constituted through historically constructed gender norms, roles, and power relations. In this view, there can be no doubt that the ethics of care must be a *feminist* ethics. As Virginia Held has argued, to accept the possibility of a nonfeminist ethics of care is to unduly disregard the history of how this ethics has developed and come to be a candidate for serious consideration among contemporary moral theories (2006: 22). Moreover, a crucial insight of care ethics as I see it is its role in the critique of the feminization and distribution of care at a variety of different levels, from the household to the level of the global political economy. These are, undeniably, feminist concerns.

These strong links to feminism have not, however, prevented various feminist and nonfeminist critics from arguing that the ethics of care is hostile to feminist goals. Because the ethics of care has been associated with women and the close personal relationships they have, especially with children, it has been interpreted as essentialist, reifying of stereotypes, and even exploitative. I argue, however, that when the ethics of care is understood as a "fully feminist" theory, these claims do not apply. From this perspective, the ethics of care is not a prescriptive ethics; indeed, while it is secure in its ontology, it lacks the normative and epistemological certainty of what Margaret Walker has called the "theoretical-juridical" model of ethics (1998: 52). Instead of prescribing "right" or "good" ethical behavior, its aim is to provide a framework for interrogating the patriarchal conditions under which values and practices associated with caring have developed in societies. It challenges the public-private dichotomy that feminizes and denigrates both caring values and caring labor and relegates them to the private realm; it argues that care is a public, political issue and an important feature of contemporary citizenship (Sevenhuijsen 1998; F. Williams 2001).

Thus, care ethics is not a "women's morality"—while it does reflect on the neglected values of care, it does not idealize caring nor assume that only women can, or should, care. On the contrary, it presents responsibilities and practices of care as the substance of morality and argues that the prevalence of women in widely undervalued caring positions is a social construction rather than a natural feature of femininity. Politically, it seeks solutions to the problems of the giving and receiving of care that are nonexploitative, equitable, and adequate to ensure the flourishing of all persons.

Care Ethics, Masculinity, and Violence

To date, most of the literature on care in the global context has focused on the implications of neoliberal globalization and its effects on the size and nature of women's care work burden (Ehrenreich and Hochschild 2002; Zimmerman, Litt, and Bose 2006). Especially prominent has been research on global care chains and the so-called global woman; this research details the experiences and effects of migrant women nannies, maids, and sex workers in the new economy (Ehrenreich and Hochschild 2002). While feminists have argued that the feminization and racialization of care in the transnational context are unjust, oppressive, and divisive for women, most of the research is driven by sociology and political economy perspectives. One recent volume aims to address the relationship between the ethics of care and global social policy surrounding care work (Mahon and Robinson, forthcoming), but by and large the ethical literature is distinct from the literature in sociology and political economy. In both fields, moreover, there has been very little work that explores the relationship between the ethics of care, masculinities, and violence.

Interrogation of the association of women with—and the detachment of men from—the values and virtues of caring is integral to the feminist enterprise. This association is central to the justification of the liberal dichotomy between the public and the private spheres and, feminists argue, has played a key role in justifying the exclusion of women from full participation in public life. The great revolution that was the birth of liberal ideas in the seventeenth century challenged the notion of patriarchal rule by asserting the fundamental equality of men based on the idea of natural rights. Knowable through reason, these rights belonged to all men and led to the birth of the idea of democracy through the heuristic device of the social contract.

While all men were seen as possessing reason and, hence, natural rights, this argument did not extend into the realm of the household. Women were not regarded at this time as the subjects of rights, and patriarchal rule within the family was left intact by early liberalism. Furthermore, the public-private became fundamental to liberalism itself. Lest this inconsistency be seen as a fatal flaw in liberalism that undermines its most basic premises, early exponents of these ideas posited a clear separation between the private sphere of the family and home and the public sphere of civic and political life. Because these two spheres were regarded as so fundamentally distinct, there was no need to ensure consistency of political ideas across them.

Thus, as feminists have pointed out, gender essentialisms and the public-private dichotomy are constitutive elements of the liberal social and political order. Moreover, since the period of industrialization, this order has existed in the West in a mutually constitutive and supportive relationship with capitalism. Here, women's caring or reproductive work, often unremunerated, enabled the productive, paid labor of "autonomous" men to continue, thus ensuring the survival of the system. Not surprisingly, feminists have focused on the implications of the liberal-capitalist order for women's exclusion from equal and full citizenship and from paid reproductive labor. Central to these arguments is the claim that in spite of the institutionalization of equal rights in most areas, many women—especially poor women of color—remain excluded and marginalized because of the structural forces and institutional effects of the pervasive public-private dichotomy.

During the first half of the twentieth century, the feminization of reproductive labor meant that care work, in the industrialized Global North, was largely unremunerated and undertaken by women in the home in the context of the nuclear family. Over the past several decades, however, there has been a partial shift toward the commodification of care work as these tasks are increasingly undertaken by migrant women. While the context of this shift is the increase in women in the North entering the paid labor force, any emancipation that these women have gained has come at an often hidden, but terrible cost. As Fiona Williams puts it, "The conditions of this work perpetuate two forms of inequality: first, the devaluation and invisibility of the private care domain and its subservience to the public world of work and, second, the translation of the unequal relations of personal interdependency into the unequal relations of transnational interdependency" (forthcoming). In spite of the high demand for care work, it remains undervalued, underresourced, and underremunerated in most societies. Because it is regarded as "undesirable work," it is available to migrant women; because it is done by poor migrant women of color—who are often subject to "racial discounting" (Ehrenreich and Hochschild 2002: 3)—this work is deemed "undesirable."

This is not to say, however, that care work is universally devalued. On the contrary, care work, especially care for children, is lauded and even venerated by certain groups in the context of the "traditional" family. The religious and political Right, including many women's organizations, upholds the traditional nuclear family and women's roles as carers, cooks, and cleaners in the home. Public care outside the home is regarded as part of the disintegration of the family and its traditional gender roles; the failings of public child care are widely seen as inherent rather than a function of underresourcing and inadequate policy and programming. The globalization of care, moreover, as described previously, is similarly deplored, but not for the inequalities it creates. Rather, the response is in line with the general backlash against migrants of color, mapped onto specific fears about the effects on traditional families of having "our children" cared for by "their women." Thus, while idealizing care work done by mothers in traditional nuclear family settings, these groups perpetuate the feminization and privatization of care work, maintaining its invisibility and shielding it from political scrutiny.

If the ethics of care is going to provide an adequate basis for understanding human security, it must interrogate the wider effects of these moral understandings. It must, for example, ask the following questions: What happens when societies feminize and devalue care and when men and masculinity are dissociated with care and relationships? How does this contribute to the construction of hegemonic forms of masculinity associated with radical individualism and different types of violence? What are the implications for security—not only for women but for communities and other social groupings? How does the focus on men's and women's roles in the context of households obscure from view the role of the structural and institutional obstacles to the creation of societies that prioritize the giving and receiving of care in an equitable and adequate manner? It is important to address the politics of masculinities and violence relating to the ethics and politics of care in order to answer these questions.

As noted earlier, while the literature on care ethics has engaged extensively with femininity and the feminization of care, it has been relatively silent on masculinity and its relationship with the values and practices of caring.[3] There are at least two reasons for this. First, in the care ethics literature, there has been a trend toward antiessentialism as feminist moral and political philosophers seek to counter the charges of essentialism often leveled at early work on care ethics, especially the work of Carol Gilligan and Nel Noddings. Second, as Virginia Held has noted, many—including many feminists—doubt that the ethics of care can appropriately address violence against women, from violence in intimate relations to the so-called public violence of wartime. She quotes Claudia Card, who argues that "attending to the kinds of violence women have suffered historically is thus important for identifying limitations of care ethics" (quoted in Held 2006: 138). As Card notes, "Women's care-taking of those who benefit from sex oppression is part of the problem that a feminist ethic needs to address" (quoted in Held 2006: 138).

Moreover, in the literature on care work, especially the literature on welfare regimes and the global care economy, emphasis is often placed on the material basis of the feminization of care—including analysis of the world of work and of the effects of neoliberal restructuring by international financial institutions. In this literature, care is widely regarded as a social and economic issue; care is analyzed as a type of labor—usually one that is under- or unremunerated and unevenly distributed along gender, and sometimes racial and class, lines. Only rarely does this literature address the values, norms, or discursive practices that underwrite and support the feminization of care work both within states and at the global level.[4]

Slowly, this neglect of images of masculinity and the activities of men is being challenged. In their study of care and welfare regimes, Paul Kershaw, Jane Pulkingham, and Sylvia Fuller argue that feminist schol-

[3] A notable exception is Kershaw, Pulkingham, and Fuller 2008.
[4] For exceptions, see F. Williams 2001; Daly 2002; and Mahon and Robinson, forthcoming.

arship must expand the subject of analysis to include "the male abuser, the promiscuous male, and the male free-rider on female care" as a primary focus of the active citizenship literature (2008: 186). The point, as Kershaw and colleagues argue, is to "interrogate cultural norms and practices which distance care provision from many social conventions that define fatherhood and masculinity" (197). This study focuses on how studies of the gendered dimensions of welfare regimes tend to rely on an "employment-oriented vision of active citizenship." The authors argue that this vision distracts attention from male violence against women and male neglect of child rearing that often precipitate entrance onto welfare for many lone mothers (182).

This argument is of great importance in that it begins to create links between the economic and physical dimensions of security—primarily, although not exclusively, for women. It is important because it demonstrates how norms surrounding the values and activities of caring constitute not only female roles that legitimize the feminization of care and care work but also masculine roles of autonomy and disconnection that may legitimize neglect or, in the worst cases, violence. The authors are careful to stress, however, that they are not proposing measures that target individual men, especially as seen in the mainstream U.S. discourse on fatherhood that focuses on poor and racialized men. Indeed, they argue that this discourse "does injustice to the scope of the problem of male irresponsibility and violence" (Kershaw, Pulkingham, and Fuller 2008: 201).

Building on this argument, I suggest that the challenge must be taken further; thus, we must not only renew our attention to "contemporary failings of fatherhood, which include violence and the patriarchal division of care" (Kershaw, Pulkingham, and Fuller 2008: 198) but also try to understand how these two "failings" are linked. In other words, the challenge is to conceptualize the ideational and material links between violence, on the one hand, and contemporary moral understandings of the values and activities of care, on the other. I do not suggest a causal or necessary connection between men's lack of involvement in caring activities and men's violence against women; I argue instead that the social norms that legitimate the former are closely connected to those that perpetuate the latter. Although the language of care may be the "different voice" of women, a critical care ethics must eschew gender essentialisms and interrogate how hegemonic forms of masculinity license men's neglect of caring responsibilities and contribute to the manipulation of images of care and womanhood into images of female subservience and sexual service.

Seen in this way, a feminist ethics of care is useful not only for highlighting women's economic insecurity but also for illuminating the relationship between the denigration of caring values and labor and the legitimation of many forms of violence—including violence against women and the masculinist "cultures" of violence that support militarism as an ideology. The reason is that it draws lines of connection between a series of apparently disparate ideological and cultural trends: neoliberal globalization, the objectification and commodification of women, the feminization of caring values and labor and the "cheapening" of care work, and constructions of hegemonic masculinity. Wresting the image of care away from its long-standing associations with the "private sphere" and "the feminine" demands a reevaluation of both femininity and masculinity. Recognizing care as a public value changes our perceptions of violence as a "natural" or necessary activity. In this sense, care is neither an antidote nor a cure for violence; indeed, prioritizing negotiation and deliberation over the place of care in societies is more likely to help prevent violent behavior. Thus, the skills acquired through caring practices—attentiveness, responsiveness, listening, and trust—may also be useful in seeking an end to violence once it has broken out and to ensuring that peace is real and enduring.

Of course, there are many dangers in isolating the problem of "male irresponsibility" in efforts to address both women's care burden and cultures of violence. In a fascinating study of the World Bank's efforts to resolve the "social reproduction dilemma" in Ecuador, Kate Bedford (2008) shows how the strategies employed—which focused on teaching men how to be responsible and reliable family members by increasing their participation in caring labor—resulted in the complete endorsement of privatized solutions to social reproduction, thus erasing child-care provision as a priority. While she acknowledges that the problems of male irresponsibility and violence are "very real," the discursive constructions of violent and lazy men in World Bank documents are both racialized and classed and are not supported by persuasive evidence (99).

The arguments about masculinity and care in this chapter should not be read as normative arguments in favor of increasing men's involvement in care work as the answer to the human insecurity caused by care deficits around the world. These kinds of claims are not only overly simplistic but also dangerous, insofar as they run the risk of leaving in place the ideological, discursive, and structural determinants of the inequalities associated with contemporary global care crises. To reiterate, the idea of hegemonic masculinities is not designed to describe the behavior or activities of individual men. On the contrary, it explains a set of fluid, socially constructed norms about "maleness" that are constituted by and embedded in social structures and institutions. While there is certainly a relationship between these norms and the behavior of some men some of the time, solutions to unequal or oppressive gender relations cannot be focused on changing men's behavior. Particular forms of masculinity must be recognized as constitutive of the wider structures and institutions, including neoliberal development policies and globalization more generally, as well as national and global cultures of militarism and military institutions. I argue that an important factor in shaping the visions of masculinity that constitute these structures and institutions is a vision of care as private and feminine. Transforming these visions of masculinity will be accomplished by focusing primarily not at the level of the household but rather at the institutions of global economic and security governance.

2 | Rethinking Human Security

Critical Security Studies

This book is not primarily a work of "security studies"; it is centrally concerned with the ways in which our normative and ontological understandings of security serve to reinforce, rather than challenge, existing relations of power, thus perpetuating and even deepening conditions of insecurity for much of the world's population. It also seeks to rethink security by examining it through the lens of a critical feminist ethics of care. In this sense, the analysis here may have links with certain branches of "critical security studies"; however, important differences should also be noted. This chapter situates my arguments regarding care and security in the context of existing debates on security—especially the critical, feminist, and human security literatures.

Critical security studies is generally assumed to have emerged as a "heterogeneous corpus of critical literature within the field of security studies in the 1990s," later solidifying into at least three distinct schools of thought: the "Copenhagen," "Aberystwyth," and "Paris" schools (c.a.s.e. collective 2006: 444). The Copenhagen school first developed the concept and theory of "securitization." This theory suggests that the act of "securitization" is primarily a discursive or speech act; it argues that security issues are the political outcome of the illocutionary force of security agents and that one of the most effective ways of analyzing security issues is through the discursive practices in different security sectors (448). The outcome of securitization is "depoliticization," in that the speech act of labeling an issue a "security issue" removes it from the realm of normal day-to-day politics, casting it as an "existential threat" and justifying extreme measures (M. Williams 1998: 435). It is argued from this perspective that these processes can have different "referent objects," depending on whether they belong to an economic, environmental, political, military, or societal sector. Of these, it is the final sector that has been the focus of attention, especially in the extent to which "identity" becomes the referent object in the societal realm.

While the Copenhagen approach to security studies could be labeled "conceptual analysis," the so-called Paris school advances security research beyond conceptual analysis. Jef Huysmans distinguishes between the conceptual analysis of the Copenhagen school and what he calls a "thick signifier" approach to security. This understanding does not assume an external reality—an "insecurity condition"—to which security refers; rather, security becomes "self-referential." It has a performative force—it organizes social relations into security relations (Huysmans 1998: 232). The thick signifier approach sets out a specific research agenda for security studies—it interprets security practices by means of interpreting the meaning of security (233). Writers from this school, which is explicitly Foucauldian in its approach, focus less on the speech act of securitization and more on the practices of "desecuritization" enacted and performed by security agencies and elites, both inside and outside the state. Of course, as argued by the c.a.s.e. collective, desecuritization, via reassuring discourses or different techniques of protection, does not always reduce insecurity or increase confidence in the political. Indeed, how security is defined conditions what is considered insecurity. Thus, policing insecurity is a mode of governmentality (c.a.s.e. collective 2006: 457).

The Aberystwyth school, by contrast, relies on a foundational moral epistemology that provides secure grounding for its normative and emancipatory claims. Concerned with addressing the "realities of security" that have been made invisible by realist security studies, critical theorists from this school seek to locate human rights abuses, the oppression of minorities, the powerlessness of the poor, and violence against women (Booth 2004: 7). The focus here is on emancipation of the individual, since emancipation, theoretically, "is security" (Booth 1991: 319). While I have no objection to these ideas as general statements of progressive goals, I am skeptical that they can provide the basis for the radical transformation that is required to achieve the kind of world that Booth has in mind. The focus on the individual as the ultimate referent for thinking about security, the reliance on human rights as the key to achieving security, and the normative commitment to cosmopolitanism do not depart sufficiently from the rhetorical and discursive logic of much liberal human security and human rights talk and, therefore, run the risk of being co-opted and diluted by state practices in much the same way as human security (see Booth 2007: 325).

The work of critical security studies scholars has provided much-needed challenges to the focus in realist security studies on states, great powers, and positivist methodologies. Of course, these three approaches do not encompass all the critical literature on security. Feminist security studies is a large and rapidly growing field (Tickner 1995, 2004; Sjoberg 2009).[1] Perspectives on security from the Global South have been a presence for decades, as have those approaches to human security informed by critical international political economy and development studies (see especially Thomas 2000). "Postcolonial" security studies is also gaining momentum (see Barkawi and Laffey 2006). My thinking about security is influenced by all of these approaches, but it is worth noting some of the differences between my approach and those just outlined.

As should be clear by now, my aim in relating the ethics and practices of care to security is not to "securitize" care, care work, or indeed, any other practices or areas of social or political life. Furthermore, my project is not oriented toward interpreting the security practices of the state or of any other institution. I am sympathetic to the arguments that security discourses may exercise power through the act of "defining" security issues and "constituting enemies" and that security practices may be read as "techniques of government." I take seriously the need

[1] On the exclusion of feminist approaches from the "critical approaches to security in Europe" network manifesto, see Sylvester 2007: 547–558.

to consider carefully invoking any notion of security—especially the human security discourse, which has been controversial on both conceptual and policy levels almost since its inception. I am wary of many critical approaches to security to the extent to which they do not leave room for the possibility of reappropriating terms (even problematic ones such as "security") and redeploying them in different contexts (c.a.s.e. collective 2006). Furthermore, many of the critical approaches, despite their critique of realism, still focus primarily on state discourse and practice, thereby obscuring the ways that gendered relations of power—often outside the state—work to silence the daily security concerns of women (see Hansen 2000, 2006; Sylvester 2007).

Methodologically, my argument does not proceed purely at the level of discourse. While it does not employ an empiricist epistemology, it does employ a feminist methodology—one that is inherently critical—in order to uncover the aspects of human social relations that are often hidden from view. Thus, I do not suggest that there is an objective, empirically verifiable "reality" of human suffering and insecurity to which our theories must refer, but I do argue that a feminist relational ontology reveals the extent to which *the continuity of life and a sense of security in people's day-to-day lives are impossible without relations and networks of care and responsibility.* In this sense, I am arguing for a shift away from understanding human security as based on the provision of individual human rights, as well as from the more critical idea of human security as a disciplining, liberal discourse. While understandings of what constitutes security are constructed by existing and dominant norms and ideologies, these understandings have real effects on the everyday well-being of people. A feminist care ethics approach to security allows us to see the effects of gender, race, class, and geopolitics in constructing accounts of security, while simultaneously revealing the fundamental importance of relations of care to the everyday security of people in their households and communities.

The reality that women—mostly women of color from income-poor countries—are responsible for most of the world's care work represents an important yet still underresearched area of global political and economic life that has bearing on the survival and day-to-day security not only of women but of all people. While development organizations and even the United Nations (UN) are beginning to recognize the importance of women and their activities to the survival and flourishing of communities around the world, security continues to be understood, theoretically, at the level of single actors—individuals, social groups, or nation-states. Changing the lens to focus not on any single actor but on the relations among those actors—relationships that are responsible for the maintenance of life itself—is important not only because it recognizes the values and activities traditionally associated with women. It also questions the denigration and feminization of these activities and demonstrates their importance to mitigating conditions of insecurity—for men and women—in a variety of contexts.

I do not deny that the reality of human insecurity itself comprises discourses that are constructed both by feminists' own concepts and by hegemonic constructions of masculinity and femininity. In this sense, security is not an objective condition that can ultimately be "achieved," since discourses—of "security," "care," and "masculinity"—are multiple, fluid, and always open to change. Even so, as discourses, all of these construct, and are constructed by, both the behaviors of real people in real social contexts and the structures and social forces that circumscribe them. The material effects, including the effects on security—of the gendered distribution of caring labor, for example—are no less real because they are discursively constructed. Furthermore, while an ethics of care, or a care ethics approach to security, cannot be "epistemologically privileged"—it does not generate principles of right or "true" moral knowledge—it can serve as a useful yardstick for illuminating both how the "reality" of security, gender relations, and care work are currently constructed and what alternative realities might look like.[2] A care ethics approach to security, I argue, disrupts existing discourses and helps to license and construct alternative discursive realities—ones that may involve less suffering and harm inflicted on people in the context of their communities.

With this in mind, my objective is to shift our gaze away from the "field" of security professionals and the practices of security toward

---

[2] The term "yardstick" is taken from Hekman's discussion of Weber's "ideal types," which she describes as "yardsticks to which reality can be compared . . . purely limiting concepts or 'utopias' . . . [which] provide a means of comparison with concrete reality in order to reveal the significance of that reality." See Hekman 1997: 361.

other kinds of practices that may appear to have no connection to security whatsoever. Here I am referring to the practices of care that sustain life in its most basic sense but also help to create a life for people that is fulfilling and rich. To focus in this way on practices of care is not to discount the importance of Foucauldian critical security studies but to allow us to see security in the context of "the everyday." From the perspective of a critical political philosophy, this task is central. I ask how practices of care—and our normative and cultural understandings of those practices—constitute the contexts circumscribing conditions of (in)security for people. In this sense, it is especially inspired by recent feminist works that seek to "engender" human security by foregrounding "the body, work and care" (Truong, Wieringa, and Chhachhi 2006) and a recent feminist study of peacekeeping, the central arguments of which draw predominantly on the ideas and practices within feminist ethics of justice and care (Porter 2006).

As Ken Booth argues in his impressive book *Theory of World Security* (2007), security must be understood as political theory. Specifically, he argues that "different attitudes and behavior associated with security are traceable to different political theories" (150). As Booth remarks, it is a simple idea with enormous implications (150). To assume, as many other critical security studies schools do, that the notion of security "carries with it a history and set of connotations that it cannot escape" prohibits the opening up of security to political theory and the politics of progressive change (165). In fact, I would go a step further to argue that while "security" may always be about the power of states and their coercive institutions for states, and for the critical social theorists who analyze their practices, it is about something entirely different for many of those people—including many women—who struggle for security for themselves and their families on a daily basis.

Human Security

Human security is an idea that emerged in the early 1990s through an unusual confluence of historical, academic, and policy developments. Central to human security is the idea that the individual must be the primary referent and beneficiary of security policy and security analysis. As Edward Newman explains, in broad terms, human security is "freedom from want" and "freedom from fear": positive and negative freedoms and rights as they relate to fundamental individual needs (2010: 78). Despite this apparently simple idea, even a brief review of the scholarly literature on human security reveals a widespread dissatisfaction with the amorphous and underdeveloped nature of the paradigm. In one of the best-known and most widely cited critiques of human security, Roland Paris makes the pithy claim that human security is like "sustainable development"—"everyone is for it, but few people have a clear idea of what it means" (2001: 88).

In spite of the diversity and ambiguity in approaches to human security, however, most formulations emphasize the welfare of ordinary people (Paris 2001: 87). In addition, most conceptions of human security are united in their rejection of the state-centrism of dominant, realist approaches to security. As Nicholas Thomas and William Tow suggest, the term "human security" has been developed as an idea that can be contrasted with "national security" and that can direct attention to an emerging and wider spectrum of security issues (2002: 178).

The origins of human security are usually traced to the 1994 UN Human Development Report, *New Dimensions of Human Security* (UNDP 1994b). This report offered a vision of security focused on individuals and groups rather than states and encompassed the dual goals of "freedom from fear" and "freedom from want" (Timothy 2004: 19). At the 2000 UN Millennium Summit, Secretary-General Kofi Annan reiterated these goals; this rearticulation of the idea of human security led to the formation of an independent Commission on Human Security. This commission, underwritten by the Japanese government, produced its final report in 2003, *Human Security Now*, which focuses on people as the main stakeholders in ensuring security and proposes a framework based upon the protection and empowerment of people (Ogata 2004: 25).

A number of national governments—notably those of Canada, Japan, and Norway—were instrumental in developing the theory of human security and promoting policy change in line with human security goals. Indeed, Canada and Norway have taken the lead in establishing a "human security network" of states and nongovernmental organizations (NGOs) that endorse the concept (Paris 2001: 87). In the academic field of international relations, research on human security has proliferated over the last decade. Theoretical approaches to human security are diverse; Owen (2004) suggests a classification of these perspectives as either narrow, focusing on political and military violence, or broad, including a range of complex issues such as poverty, disease, health, and the environment. Scholars of human security have also been influenced by a wide variety of theoretical and methodological perspectives, including critical theory (Dunne and Wheeler 2004; Booth 1991, 1997), constructivism (Newman 2001), critical international political economy (Thomas 2000; Thomas and Wilkin 1999), and liberalism (Axworthy 1997, 2001).

While there are many criticisms of the idea of human security that revolve around its conceptual "fuzziness" and its normative idealism, I am more concerned with critiques that surround its effects on reinforcing, rather than challenging, existing relations of power in world politics. The idea that invoking human security could lead to more traditional security practices—including militarized practices—thus potentially making humans less secure, is a serious problem that warrants careful consideration. This idea is addressed in both the securitization argument—which suggests that "speaking" security leads to a process of depoliticization and the increase of executive or emergency powers and, often, military force—and the thick signifier approach, which argues that policing insecurity is a mode of governmentality; in the latter approach, securitization means the capacity to control borders, manage threats, define endangered identities, and delineate the spheres of order (c.a.s.e. 2006: 457). These kinds of analyses are both illuminating and convincing in the contexts of terrorism and the "war on terror" as well as in relating to issues concerning the security practices of border control, including surveillance and other forms of policing. They also can be seen in the discourse and practices of the UN in the context of global governance where, as Hans-Martin Jaeger has argued, "human security transformed global governance into a project of individual self-government in everyday life, irrespective of the political conditions circumscribing the latter" (2007: 264).

In sum, critics suggest that human security is inherently tied to liberal visions of good governance. Neoliberal economic reform has reinforced the status quo, thereby failing to recognize the extent to which the ideological and structural features of the global political economy may, in fact, reduce rather than enhance the security of individuals. Related to this is the argument that, rather than represent a radical shift, human security has provided a justification for the use of traditional security practices—including military intervention—in the name of "higher" moral purposes. These are usually understood as those articulated in internationally recognized standards of human rights and governance; in this sense, most human security scholarship is explicitly or implicitly underpinned by a solidarist commitment, and some is cosmopolitan in ethical orientation (Newman 2010: 78).

This book is, in part, a response to these critiques and grows out of dissatisfaction with the existing conceptualizations of human security and the ethics on which they are based. As I have argued elsewhere, in the fields of international relations and human security, these ethical approaches—namely, solidarist or cosmopolitan approaches to human rights and justice—are often insufficiently reflective on the extent to which their core values may reproduce dominant norms and existing power relations in the current world order (F. Robinson 2008: 168). Focusing on freedoms—whether from "fear" or "want"—privileges the individual and obscures from view structural determinants, institutional constraints, and social relations of power. While critical analyses of human security have interrogated these wider structures of power in the context of the global political economy (Thomas 2000; O'Manique 2006), there has been less attention paid to the structural, institutional, and ideational factors that contribute to cultures of militarism and those that privilege violent solutions to social and political conflict.

Human rights are widely cited in the human security literature as the normative foundation for human security. They provide both the moral basis on which to build accounts of human security—relying on universalist notions of human dignity—and the key to the realization of human security. Indeed, it could be said that the purpose of thinking about human security is to elucidate in a meaningful and contemporary manner the threats and risks that currently challenge the universal enjoyment of human rights. But rights-based ethics are conceptually and morally problematic for a number of reasons. This is not to say that rights, and the freedoms they seek to protect, are not important; rather, it is to suggest that the concept of rights alone may not be able to do the "moral work" that it needs to in order to provide a complete ethics (see

F. Robinson 1998). This is the case despite the fact that many groups—including especially women's groups and feminists—have worked hard, and with considerable success, to "rethink" the concept of rights so that it can address their needs, concerns, and interests (see F. Robinson 2003).

Dominant approaches to rights—including rights as they are widely conceptualized and articulated by Western states, international organizations, and large Western civil society groups—are most often based on an ontology of atomistic individualism that privileges the norm of self-sufficiency and neglects the relational nature of human existence and the fundamental nature of the human need to give and receive adequate care.[3] This ontology further privileges a masculinized understanding of power as residing in the state, thus neglecting relations of power based on gender, race, and class. In articulating a set of universalized "principled norms," human rights and human security approaches tend to focus on international law and the macropicture of global governance, thereby neglecting the ways in which both state power and contemporary global governance actually play out in the particular contexts of households and communities. Finally, while universal human rights as political theory or international law may provide us with a "shopping list" of necessary conditions of human flourishing, when dominant approaches to human rights are played out in the political arena—as they always are—they rarely provide an alternative discourse or normative orientation through which to challenge the hegemonic ideology of neoliberalism.

Gender, Feminism, and Human Security

Not surprisingly, feminists have generally welcomed the human security approach. As Kristen Timothy suggests, feminists have been attracted to the potential of the human-security paradigm for linking a range of women's activist concerns into an integrated strategy for gender justice (2004: 22). In theoretical terms, moreover, the source of the alliance is

---

[3] The work of feminist philosophers, political theorists, and legal theorists has been crucial in rethinking the idea of rights so that it takes account more fully of relationality and context. See, for example, Gould 2004.

evident: Both feminist security studies and human security approaches reject the dominant realist, state-centric approaches to national security that privilege the security of the state from the threat of external violence. Both argue that the dominant approaches ignore the causes of *human* insecurity—including those caused by economic, environmental, and social threats, the source of which may come from within the state or, indeed, from the state itself. Because the individual becomes the primary referent of security, and the state is seen as a potential threat, the realization of individual human rights is often regarded as the analytical and substantive key to achieving human security.

In spite of these shared commitments, however, feminists have also been quick to point out the gender blindness in the theory of human security. It has been suggested that, in spite of the broad and inclusive nature of the human security approach, the gender dimension tends to be overlooked. For example, two prominent scholar-activists for women's human rights—Charlotte Bunch and Mary Robinson—have argued that the human rights focus of human security is to be welcomed, as long as a "feminist human rights lens" is used to foreground the particular threats to security faced by women. As Robinson (2005) suggests, for women, gender is itself a risk factor threatening human security. Both Bunch and Robinson are aware of the multiple risks faced by women—including poverty, lack of property and reproductive rights, and political exclusion; yet both also highlight the particular problem of violence against women. Indeed, Bunch argues that there is no better paradigm for human security than violence against women, which affects vast numbers of women and can feed acceptance of violence as an inevitable and normal means of dealing with differences (2004: 32–33).

It is important to note, as Bunch does, that the 2003 report of the Commission on Human Security does integrate gender-based inequality and violence into the topics raised in the report. It also recognizes that women are often responsible for holding family and community together and have, in that regard, played important roles in addressing armed conflict and poverty (Bunch 2004: 32–33). Indeed, the commission cochair, Sadako Ogata, has defended its approach, arguing that the decision not to isolate women as a special area of concern, as a category of victims of conflict, or as instruments of development reflected its view that gender-based inequality and violence cut across all matters relating to human security. Furthermore, Ogata argues that this approach also reflected the commission's desire to avoid portraying women as victims and instead to highlight the ways in which women have used their power for preventing conflict prevention and reducing poverty (2004: 27).

Feminist critics, however, have questioned the adequacy of this approach. Kristen Timothy, for example, argues that in spite of the apparent commitment of the commission to women and gender, the final report included only a few examples of women's security issues, including critical human security concerns for women, such as violence against women in the family (2004: 23). Charlotte Bunch emphasizes this omission, describing it as an illustration of her main concern with the approach of the commission, specifically that by not taking up women as a specific subject, the report fails to fully explore complex issues of bodily integrity that women have identified as critical to their intimate security: reproductive rights and violence against women (2004: 32). She says women should be taken up in human security dialogue as a "subject or constituency" so that we can address issues that predominantly affect women (32).

These important feminist arguments challenge the assumption that rights, and threats to those rights, apply universally to the ungendered "human" subject. Yet I question two aspects of this approach. First, while Bunch specifically refers to her argument as "feminist," the focus on women as a constituency or group of individual women sets up women in opposition to men, maintaining the dichotomous ontologies that many feminists seek to overcome. This focus on women, moreover, can only ever provide a partial conceptualization of human security— one that is relevant only to women. Second, I argue that the continued reliance on individual human rights—albeit women's individual human rights—may be problematic if the goal is to understand *how people actually experience threats to their security* and what kinds of policy measures could help achieve security for some of the world's most vulnerable people.

Not all feminists, however, are wedded to the human rights approach to human security. Indeed, a number of feminists have explored the implications of gender for human security by elaborating critical feminist theories of human security that focus on *context* and *relationality.* Gunhild Hoogensen and Kristi Stuvoy, for example, argue that the meaning of security becomes clear only *according to the context* (2006: 221). One of the potential benefits of human security, they suggest, is that it can direct analytical attention to security as a "life-world phenomenon in a societal context"; moreover, while human security may be vested in individuals, it is "realized intersubjectively in specific local contexts" (221). In particular, they stress that human security must be conceptualized in terms of relationships of dominance and nondominance that determine who defines norms and practices and who must follow them. Analyses of security, then, must explore how these practices were constituted, naturalized, and reconstituted (219, 224).

Similarly, Heidi Hudson questions the term "human" in human security; collapsing femininity or masculinity into the term "human," she argues, could conceal the gendered underpinnings of security practices. This is also the case in the presentation of "women" as a group (Hudson 2005: 157). Hudson emphasizes the need to redefine power in "relational" terms, thereby recognizing that in many cases "the survival of one depends on the well-being of the other" (156). As Laura Sjoberg argues, a feminist approach to security recognizes human security not as individual security but as social security (2009: 206). This is emphasized most explicitly by Thanh-Dam Truong, Saskia Wieringa, and Amrita Chhachhi, who argue that

> the human security approach has yet to free itself from the regnant tendency in neo-liberal reforms which tends to apply primarily male norms in valuing and regulating social life, obliterating the significance of arrangements which provide care for the very young, sick and elderly. . . . For all the pronouncements about women, children and the elderly as social groups vulnerable to human security threat, the global reality . . . tells another story, and brings home the message that these tendencies may reflect a deep crisis in care systems worldwide. (2006: xxi).

These critical interventions suggest a more promising approach to feminist human security than the human rights–based conceptions of Bunch and Robinson. Indeed, relationality and context, which are key features of their arguments, are also two crucial aspects of critical care ethics. I now begin to sketch out how these ideas relating feminist ethics to security may be developed through a critical analysis of the gendered effects of contemporary globalization.

Security through the Lens of Care

Attention to the practices and discourses surrounding care leads us not only to recognize the addition of a new human security "issue" but rather to rethink both the meaning of and ways of achieving human security for women as well as for most of the world's people. Dominant understandings of human security have privileged the autonomous individual as the primary referent of security, while focusing almost exclusively on individual human rights in the context of liberal "good governance" (see Axworthy 2001; Commission on Human Security 2003).[4] There is little or no recognition of the extent to which our attitudes toward care—how important it is, who should do it—shape our understandings of human security and insecurity. For example, key human security documents, such as *Human Security Now*, overemphasize waged work and neglect care, addressing it only indirectly at best (Truong, Wieringa, and Chhachhi 2006: xix).

In this sense, my approach offers a fundamentally new way of looking at the debate within critical security studies regarding the primary referent or referents of security. A critical ethics of care disrupts and challenges the dichotomy between the individual and the collective. What becomes important, then, is not articulating whether individuals, families, communities, ethnic groups, societies, states, or the world should be the referents of security; rather, the key is the ontological argument that all human beings exist at a fundamental level in relation to others. This is not a superficial empirical claim that refers to "connections" between people; on the contrary, it is a philosophical claim about the constitution of subjectivity through relations. To say that our "existence" is relational refers both to ourselves as moral, social, and

---

[4] Critical work on human security eschews these links between human security, liberalism, and global governance, asking instead in whose interests global governance and the policies of neoliberalism are operating and whether they are in fact supportive of human security. See especially Thomas 2001: 159–175.

political subjects and to the ontological basis of human life—from survival to flourishing. In security terms, it means that we cannot simply look at entities—individuals, societies, states—as if they are preformed and autonomous. Individuals exist in relation to other individuals and groups; these relations are subject to change and are saturated with different forms and levels of power. To consider, and seek to address, an individual's security, we must understand the relational context. In particular, concern for the security of people must have as its central focus concerns for the state of relations of responsibility and care. These relations are the basis of human security. Relations of care will exist at a variety of different levels—from the household, to international governmental and nongovernmental organizations. The division of care among these different groups will vary from society to society and will be affected by a wide variety of cultural factors. It is neither possible nor desirable to prescribe what adequate care or a just distribution of care work would look like across all geographic and cultural contexts. But as the following chapters demonstrate, security of bodies in terms of health and bodily integrity and economic security in terms of the ability to work and provide for families demand attention to the nature, levels, and resources of care provided and to the distribution, nature, and amount of care work undertaken. As I have suggested, the "reality" of conditions surrounding care is constituted by discourses of gender, race, and class, as well as by ideological dichotomies of Left and Right, public and private, and masculine and feminine. It is also embedded in the material relations and structural features that constitute the contemporary global political economy.

Women, men, and children exist in relationships in all societies that frame their experiences of insecurity. Different races and ethnic groups exist in relationships in the context of households, communities, and states and at the global level. Relationships among states and their constituent groups in the global political economy are characterized by webs of dependence and interdependence—increasingly in ways that defy dominant discourses of dependency in world politics. Relationships of responsibility and care determine who takes up arms in political conflicts and who receives crucial medication and care in conditions of scarcity of resources and time. While scholars of international relations have begun to broaden security by exploring the security implications of issues like poverty and health, they have remained silent on the effects of poverty, environmental degradation, and health pandemics on our ability to provide care for those in need or of the potential of a critical ethics of care to serve as a moral framework for these security crises. Indeed, there is a dearth of research on these issues in any field of study, although some work is emerging from within gender studies, sociology, and social policy studies (see especially Zimmerman, Litt, and Bose 2006).

For example, in her excellent analysis of women's care work in post-Soviet Azerbaijan, Mehrangiz Najafizadeh highlights many of the untold consequences of violent conflict on families and caregiving. Importantly, her analysis focuses not on the conflict in isolation; rather, she explores the Nagorno-Karabakh conflict with Armenia in the context of post-Soviet economic, political, and social transformation. Najafizadeh explains how and why caregiving responsibilities have increased in this context. Of course, the conflict alone has multiple effects: Many people are acutely injured or physically disabled by war; in particular, many women lose their husbands or sons to the fighting, which has obvious effects on the burden of care. An increase in the number of orphans is also a direct cause of war. In Azerbaijan, a combination of Azeri tradition and macroeconomic constraints dictates that female members of the orphan's extended family, rather than the state, provide care for the child (Najafizadeh 2003: 297). These children require not only physical care but also emotional caregiving in the light of the trauma they have experienced. Moreover, many of these children, like the women who are caring for them, are refugees who have been uprooted from their homes and communities and are living in tents or in railroad boxcars (297). All of this is exacerbated by the social and economic effects of global restructuring in the post-Soviet context: increased unemployment in the formal sector among women and men; men leaving their wives and family to seek work in another area; increased numbers of women working in the informal sector; the elimination of state services—including day cares, kindergartens, and state medical services and state-funded pensions for the elderly (296).

Of course, women are not just passive observers to economic restructuring or to men's political violence; indeed, they may be directly involved as fighting soldiers or "camp followers," as victims of rape or domestic violence, or as global commodities—domestic or sex workers—to be bought, sold, and trafficked across borders. In all of these cases of violence and exploitation, however, women's agency must be recognized; many women claim the "right to fight" and struggle for recognition and equality within their militaries; moreover, the "global women" who leave their homes, and often their children, to find work abroad as nannies do so to provide a better life for themselves and the families they leave behind. At the same time, however, it is important to recognize that women's (and men's) agency is constrained by the gendered norms, institutions, and structures of militarism and neoliberal global restructuring. Female soldiers may be prevalent in many countries—including a number of African countries—but their decisions to join their militaries must be interrogated critically. As Susan McKay and Dyan Mazurana show in their study of girl soldiers in Africa, for many, joining is a response to violence against themselves or their community, a protection strategy or an opportunity to meet their basic needs. Others enter through being abducted by members of the armed forces (McKay and Mazurana 2004). Similarly, migrant women are often driven out of desperation to use illegal channels to cross borders. Women and children who are forced into labor and sexual exploitation often fear arrest or deportation if they contact authorities regarding their situations (Fukuda-Parr 2004: 38). Migrant sex workers are frequently motivated by the need to manage an overwhelming burden of care (see Hankivsky, forthcoming).

Recognition of structural and institutional contexts is also crucial when we consider the politics of the natural environment. When we examine the effects of environmental disasters—floods, earthquakes, hurricanes, and tsunamis—we may recognize the natural cause but must also understand the social and political significance. The World Health Organization (WHO) reports that women and children are particularly affected by disasters, accounting for more than 75 percent of displaced persons. As described previously in the case of war, gender roles dictate that women become the primary caretakers for those affected by disasters, substantially increasing their emotional and material workload (WHO 2009). In addition to suffering the general effects of natural disasters and lack of health care, women are vulnerable to reproductive and sexual health problems and increased rates of sexual and domestic violence (WHO 2009). This situation mirrors that of violent conflict, where increased gender-based and sexual violence are accompaniments to rising poverty and the collapse of social safety nets (Fukuda-Parr 2004: 41).

A similar mix of an unmanageable burden of care with poverty and the potential for violence can be seen in the context of global HIV/ AIDS. Over 2 million children and 31 million adults are infected with HIV worldwide (UNAIDS 2009). While AIDS is obviously a reality for families and individuals throughout the world, its presence in some parts of sub-Saharan Africa almost defies comprehension. Indeed, it is believed that 70 percent of all HIV cases in the world are located within the area (Kayumba 2000: 447). In Botswana, for example, an estimated 39 percent of reproductive-age adults are infected with HIV (UNESCO 2003).

Global attention to this crisis has been sorely lacking. As Fukuda-Parr argues, the threat to human security poised by HIV/AIDS does not stop with the individuals who are ill and die but extends to their families and communities (2004: 40). Of the important challenges raised by the pandemic, moreover, those related to care and care work have been most consistently overlooked. In her analysis of the role of women as caregivers in Tanzania, Akwilina Kayumba (2000) argues that despite the fact that more and more women are entering the labor market and struggling to maintain flexibility in the roles as workers and caregivers, Tanzanian society at large still expects women to stop working and take care of sick relatives when the need arises. This expectation, which can be explained by reference to both economic factors and religious/cultural norms, has a number of consequences. Taking care of a sick HIV relative is not a short-term prospect; indeed, an infected person requires ongoing care until he or she dies. A working woman charged with this task will need extended time off from her employer in order to stay with the patient or prepare food and feed the patient. Moreover, women are physically vulnerable, insofar as they are ignorant of the risks involved, and they suffer mental stress by sharing the suffering of their sick relatives (Kayumba 2000: 447).

As Jody Heymann argues, one of the most important challenges is how to raise healthy children while at the same time address the needs of those adults and children already infected. In a study conducted in

Botswana, Heymann found that, in the absence of adequate child care for HIV-infected children when they become sick, parents must provide care. The study showed that 29 percent of such parents left work at least once a month to attend sick children; this led to loss of income and, at times, loss of job (Heymann 2003b). Moreover, even children who are not themselves HIV infected are deeply affected by the disease if their parents become sick or if their parents have to care for others who are sick. Quite simply, HIV/AIDS caregiving—much of which is done by women—affects the ability of those parents to provide routine care for children who are not infected (Heymann 2003b).

All of this, in all of its messy, exhaustingly relentless reality, is the permanent background to the "heavyweight" moral and political issues related to globalization of human rights and human security. The widely recognized aspects of human security—freedom from poverty, food security, health care and protection from disease, protection from environmental pollution and depletion, physical safety from violence and survival of traditional cultures—cannot be realized in the absence of robust, equitable, well-resourced relations and networks of care at the household, community, state, and transnational levels. Moreover, none of these "goods" are achieved or enjoyed by individuals in isolation from others and the networks of care and support they provide. Relations and networks of care, for example, determine responsibilities for how food is prepared and distributed within households. Access to health care depends upon prior commitments to ensure adequate care; states, communities, and households must negotiate responsibilities for care and make decisions about who will provide that care, what that care will look like, and how that care will be resourced. The trajectory of the global political economy for the last several decades has been driven by the devaluation, feminization, and privatization of caring services; most recently, globalization has been literally supported by the transnationalization of caring and "intimate" labor. I argue that this context has not, and cannot be, one in which adequate levels of human security can be achieved and sustained.

While households must make moral decisions about the organization of care, so, too, must communities and nation-states. Moreover, these decisions are always made within the constraints and context of global economic governance, geopolitics, and "cultural" norms about gender, race, and the role and nature of caring. From the perspective of a critical feminist ethics of care, these moral decisions cannot and should not be made without careful considerations of the specific social and personal relations and how each will be affected. Determining the nature, amount, and distribution of care at these different levels is not merely a question of distributive justice. As Joan Tronto (forthcoming) has argued, we need to recall that politics is about power not only in this distributive sense but also in the sense of the creation or assumption of collective capacity to act. Our most basic ideas about care will shape our assumptions about the scope and limit of responsibilities related to care. Policy on care connects in fundamental ways with values and norms and the organization of society itself (Daly 2002: 268). Determining responsibilities for care in particular cases will involve consideration, and sometimes critical interrogation of, existing social norms and values. Moreover, from the perspective of care ethics, ensuring human security in the context of HIV/AIDS devastation requires consideration of "those experiencing the set of needs embodied in care and the actors who seek or are assigned to satisfy those needs" (Daly 2002: 268).

Perhaps most important, we must remember that complex relations of power shape these moral scenes. In the words of Margaret Walker, morality itself is a "disposition of powers through an arrangement of responsibilities" (2003: 106). These powers include those constituted through gender relations and through relations of race, class, age, and ability. Norms of hegemonic masculinities are implicated in intimate relations as well as embedded in the structures and institutions of the global political economy. The ways in which care and care work are valued and distributed at a variety of levels—from the household to the global political economy—provide the context through which questions of ethics and human security must be viewed.

Considering human security through the lens of care ethics focuses our attention differently. This approach demands greater consideration of the particular contexts in which people are experiencing insecurity. Who—which humans—are experiencing insecurity? How does the relational context of their lives affect the nature of their insecurity? What combination of resources, services, and time (to care) will help achieve more secure households and communities? How does the wider socioeconomic context—at the national and global levels—work either with or against the goal of creating a sense of security among people in the context of their relationships and communities? This context includes existing cultural norms on gender relations, race, and ethnicity, as well as existing political culture on the legitimacy of care and the balance of the role of the state and private institutions—including the household—in providing that care.

Toward a Feminist Theory of Human Security

In spite of their diversity, current approaches to human security are united by their lack of attention to the values and practices of care and caregiving. This neglect is linked to their reliance on the "ungendered" human being as the primary referent of human security, as well as to the rights-based normative framework on which human security relies. A critical, feminist ethics of care can provide an alternative normative basis for human security—one that relies on a relational ontology and that allows space for critical interrogation of relations of gender and race.

In the context of global politics, a feminist ethics of care rejects the traditional focus on individuals, states, and institutions as autonomous actors and the attention only to macrolevel regimes and processes in the evaluation of globalization and human security. In contrast to this approach is one that sees individuals as existing in complex webs of interconnection—in families, neighborhoods, ethnic and religious groups— since it is in this context that their feelings of security or insecurity are actually played out in particular lived experiences. This approach would recognize the importance of care as a fundamental aspect of human flourishing, as well as the need to preserve and facilitate good caring relations, while refusing to valorize or idealize care. It would also examine care as a practice and a kind of work and interrogate how decisions about the distribution of care are made in any given social context. Only after gaining some understanding of responsibility and power at this level can we then make sense of the relationship between the policies of states and institutions and people's daily lives.

A recognition of the full implications of care ethics as a lens through which to view security leads to the revision of our objectives beyond the delivery of rights narrowly understood, toward a recognition of responsibilities and need for care. Of course, the critical and transformative power of rights language should not be underestimated; there is a need, however, to move beyond rights as the sole normative, transformative idea. Indeed, we should begin to think about how rights may, for example, serve as an immediate strategy for those who are vulnerable and dispossessed to draw attention to their plight and to secure the conditions for independence; the ethics of care, then, could guide us in the longer term, based on the conviction that the needs and interests of all people would be better served in societies that valued interdependence and acknowledged the vulnerability of all (F. Williams 2001: 481). The discourse of individual rights cannot, alone, effectively address the complex sets of relations that both lead to situations of human insecurity and can ultimately find lasting solutions to that insecurity. This in no way suggests that the recognition of political freedom from the coercive power of the state is in some way unimportant or that the demands of justice—especially those that recognize human autonomy and political freedom—should be ignored. Rather, this approach argues that human autonomy can be achieved only through good relations of care and that justice and political freedom can be enjoyed only under conditions where care is adequate and given without exploitation or marginalization.

3 | "Women's Work"

The Global Care and Sex Economies

*A global demand exists for labour whose core component consists
of "women's work." By this I mean sex, childcare and housework.*
—MACKLIN 2003

This chapter explores the human security dimensions of "women's work" in the global economy through the lens of a critical feminist ethics of care. By "women's work" I mean care work (including child care and care for the sick and elderly); household maintenance labor (including cleaning and food preparation); and "intimate" labor (including prostitution, other forms of sex work, and "mail-order brides"). Currently, millions of women from income-poor, peripheral states migrate to more affluent countries to do the work that is "associated with a wife's traditional role—child care, homemaking and sex" (Ehrenreich and Hochschild 2002: 4). This situation is usually linked causally to recent social and demographic transformations in the nature, extent, and location of paid work; the most striking and influential of these demographic shifts has been the increase in women in the paid workforce. Ehrenreich and Hochschild report that recent estimates show women as the sole, primary, or coequal earners in more than half of American families (2002: 3); in Canada, between 1960 and 2000, the female share of the labor force increased from 25 to 48 percent (Heymann et al. 2004: 4).

In income-rich countries, in the absence of accessible, affordable, universal child-care programs, many women working outside the home now purchase transnationally the reproductive labor that they no longer have time to provide. Between 1985 and 1990, the number of women migrating to another country increased at a faster rate than the number of men (UNIFEM 2000: 31). By the beginning of the twenty-first century, women made up almost 50 percent of the world's 120 million migrants, many of them seeking reproductive work in the nearest comparatively rich country (Agathangelou 2004: 5). In countries like the Philippines, Indonesia, and Sri Lanka, female migrant workers significantly outnumber men (UNIFEM 2005). While the focus of this migration tends to be on nannies and domestic workers, the migration of women for sex work is a substantial part of this trend. As Agathangelou points out, "desire industries" constitute one of the fastest-growing employment sectors for working-class migrant women (2004: 6).

Both the "pull" and "push" sides of these migration flows reveal a growing crisis of care in both the Global North and the Global South. In the income-rich North, care gaps are left as more women enter or reenter the paid labor force. In the South, countries are still struggling to accommodate the conditions of neoliberal economic globalization, including structural adjustment programs (SAPs), the opening of their economies to foreign firms, and International Monetary Fund (IMF) austerity measures following financial crises (Sassen 2002: 257). Meanwhile, many women in developing economies are struggling to find ways to support themselves and their families, in the light of reduced employment opportunities for men and women and cutbacks in social services linked to the burden of debt servicing. This chapter addresses the human security dimensions of women's transnational labor in the global economy. I argue, first, that the increase in legal and illegal migration flows of women interact with structures of gender equality at every level—global, national, communal, and familial (Heyzer 2006: 102)—and that this creates the potential for enormous insecurity for those women. This insecurity has both economic and physical dimensions. Although many women migrate in order to pursue economic opportunities that may improve their overall economic security, this usually comes at a cost. In many countries, substandard employment practices and the use of undocumented workers can lead to the concealing of workers by employers through physical confinement. Because they work in private homes, domestic workers are particular vulnerable to overwork or physical and sexual abuse. Finally, women who are pushed toward trafficking for sex work as an alternative to the drudgery and danger that characterizes their daily lives at home are particularly vulnerable to myriad physical and mental health problems, including HIV/AIDS, sexually transmitted diseases (STDs), and unwanted pregnancies (Heyzer 2006: 107–109).

Second, by employing a critical feminist ethics of care as an ontological and normative lens through which to view the human security dimensions of women's transnational reproductive labor, I use the context of women's migrant and trafficked labor to illustrate why human security must be understood *relationally*. I argue that the concept of the global care chain provides an excellent tool for highlighting the relational nature of human security in this context. The concept of the global care chain refers to "a series of personal links between people across the globe based on the paid or unpaid work of caring" (Hochschild 2000: 131). In Hochschild's original formulation, the concept typically entails "an older daughter from a poor family who cares for her siblings while her mother works as a nanny caring for the children of a migrating nanny who, in turn cares for the child of a family in a rich country" (131).

As Nicola Yeates argues, global care chains do not simply demonstrate the connections between personal lives and global politics; they elucidate the structures and processes that reflect and perpetuate the unequal distribution of resources globally (2004: 373). I also argue that the concept demonstrates clearly the extent to which the human security of women, children, and entire families is linked in a complex relational ontology that often crosses regional and state boundaries. To put it simply, the human security of children and families in many income-poor countries cannot be considered independently from the security of migrating or trafficked women who have left them behind. These relationships, furthermore, must be understood as embedded in both the institutions and structures of the global care economy and in the gender and racial norms and hierarchies that feminize and devalue caring labor. Indeed, the human security impact of migrant care work is of greater significance in the light of Yeates's argument that the concept of the global care chain should be expanded to include other groups of migrant care workers—such as nurses—in different care contexts over different historical periods (2004: 374).

As I have argued previously in this book, a critical ethics of care does not valorize caring relations or caring values as essentially "feminine," intrinsically morally superior, or more desirable based on their "femininity." On the contrary, it is essentially a set of claims about how moral responsibilities and practices arise and about the nature and substance of morality. By locating moral responsibilities and the practices that seek to fulfill them, care ethics focuses on ontology. Specifically, this lens focuses our attention on the subjects of security as beings-in-relation; the degree and nature of insecurity of most individual human beings are intimately connected to the lives and security of others. Moreover, it allows us to see the extent to which all persons rely on adequate care as a fundamental condition of survival and security. As care becomes transnationalized, the webs of relations that provide care and security become more complex. As care is increasingly commodified, feminized, and racialized, its links to security demand attention to transnational hierarchies of gender and race, the normative structures of hegemonic masculinities, and the moralized discourses of "womanhood," "family," "exoticism," and "national security." A feminist ethics of care can thus help to uncover and elucidate the normative discourses and structures that govern the global distribution of "intimate services" and of responsibilities and demand for those services. Moreover, as a feminist ethics, it can assist in revealing the reasons *why* women, especially women of color, are responsible for sex work, as they are for housework and care work, and why there is relatively little critical moral reflection on this in the context of relations of gender and race at the global level.

Thus, I explore the global crisis of care in the context of the contemporary global political economy. In an effort to demonstrate the human security costs of this crisis, and the relational nature of those human security effects, I examine the coping strategies of women and families, especially in developing countries. For women in the income-rich Global North, coping with the "care gap" often involves employing migrant domestic workers from developing countries. It is crucial to address not only the insecurity experienced by these migrant women but also that experienced by others in the global care chain—including dependent children—that they leave behind. Finally, I explore the ethical and security dimensions of sex workers. I argue that although there are obvious differences between the activities of trafficked sex workers and migrant child-care workers, both must be understood in the context of gendered and racialized processes in the contemporary global political economy. Furthermore, I argue that sex workers show us, in Olena Hankivsky's words, the "dark side of care" (forthcoming) and that a feminist ethics of care can help us to understand both the motivations of sex workers and the implications of this work for human security.

The Crisis of Care and the Transnationalization of Care Work

All over the world, demographic and social transformations have altered the nature, extent, and location of paid work. These changes began in the mid-nineteenth century in North America and Europe, as men, and then women, moved into the industrial and postindustrial workforces, but the changes have now occurred and are continuing to take place worldwide (Heymann et al. 2004: 3). The urbanization of the global population—from 18 percent at the beginning of the twentieth century to nearly 50 percent at the end—has led to important changes in community, work, and family life, including the inability of extended families to live together and the need for more adult family members to take up paid employment away from the home (4). But perhaps the most striking demographic shift has been the increase in women in the paid workforce: In Kuwait, the increase was from 4 to 31 percent. In many other regions, including southern Africa, the female participation in the labor force was already well over 40 percent in 1960 and remained high in 2000 (Heymann et al. 2004: 3–4). In 2003, 1.1 billion of the world's 2.8 billion workers, or 40 percent, were women, representing a worldwide increase of nearly 200 million women in employment in the past ten years (ILO 2004).

This trend is occurring concurrently with exponential growth in the global population. Although the number of children per family has dropped in both the industrial, and much of the developing, world since the 1970s, 77 million people continue to be added to the world every year (Radford Ruether 2005: 23). As Rosemary Radford Ruether notes, Western concerns with population have usually ignored the gender dimension of this question. Women bear the children and do most of the caretaking (23). In the industrialized North, and in the absence of accessible, affordable, universal child-care programs, women working outside the home have turned to poor women of color—often immigrant women—to care for their children. These women may be citizens or permanent residents of these industrialized countries, or they may be "illegal aliens"; they may even be migrants participating in schemes to bring female domestic workers to the North from countries such as the Philippines. Between 1985 and 1990, the number of women migrating to another country increased at a faster rate than the number of men (UNIFEM 2000: 21).

In parts of the Global South, the recent acceleration of these twin trends of urbanization and rising paid labor force—with most notable rises in female participation—can be explained partly by the nature of economic globalization or, more specifically, global economic restructuring.[1] In this era of accelerated speed and scope of global trade and investment, states compete fiercely to provide a low-cost economic environment that is attractive to investors. This has often meant the relocation of production processes to the Global South, where regulations are minimal and wages and working conditions are poor. Women for the most part have taken up these new "opportunities" in export sectors, which has meant long hours working outside the home. Moreover, while social programs have been under fire for decades all over the world, the power of international financial institutions in developing countries has meant that the erosion of state-run welfare provision is felt the hardest there. Women—already overburdened with labor responsibilities—must fill in the gaps. When all adults within a household work outside the home for pay, obvious and often serious problems arise. Financial responsibilities must be balanced with caregiving responsibilities, especially where care is required for children; elderly, infirm, or disabled adults; and acutely or chronically ill family members.

Moreover, while these trends are evident throughout the world, it is important to consider the differential effects of these changes on working families in the Global North and the Global South. In many cases, women's entry into the paid labor force in the Global North represents

---

[1] On the difference between "globalization" and "global restructuring," see Marchand and Runyan 2000.

an exercise of "choice" and a desire for financial independence and the satisfaction that work can bring. This is not to diminish the extent to which many women in the North work outside the home first and fore-most due to financial need; indeed, this is especially true in the case for female-headed, single-parent families. But all of these women, regard-less of their socioeconomic circumstances, require care for their children when they work outside the home—except in those increasing but still rare cases where men cease their work outside the home to take on the role of primary caregiver. Ironically, while it is important to recognize that women in the North often work outside the home because of finan-cial need, it is also the case that many women *give up* their paid labor to care for their children because child care is too expensive. In other words, financial need forces them to leave their jobs—which they may enjoy and value—because the cost of child care, especially for a num-ber of children, is prohibitive. This in itself demonstrates a disjuncture between the needs and rights of women and the role and policies of wealthy Western states in the current era.

In parts of the Global South, structural adjustment policies and development programs have propelled a global increase in women's employment in the low-wage service sector (Litt and Zimmerman 2003: 157). The increased concentration of women in manufacturing work in the South certainly raises women's earnings; however, this work is usu-ally inflexible with regard to hours and incompatible with child supervi-sion (Glick 2003: 148). Moreover, the dependence of third-world states on international financial institutions has weakened state provisions for health, education, and social services, placing an increased burden on women's unpaid labor—or care work—in the home (Litt and Zimmer-man 2003: 157). While the causes and circumstances of the increase in women's paid labor in the South differ from those of women in the North, the effects are also dramatically different.

First, and most obviously, the households in the South are trying to meet their caregiving needs with far fewer resources. While many working women in the North are confronted with real choices regarding work and care, many women of the South have no choice. This means, in simple terms, that they must work for wages or they and their chil-dren will not survive; often, this means they are forced to leave small children home alone and unsupervised because they cannot afford to pay for child care. Second, the age-dependency ratios—of children and elderly to working-age adults—tend to be 50–100 percent higher in the developing world than in developing countries (Heymann, Fischer, and Engelman 2003: 77). Thus, the burden is already significantly heavier, simply due to demographic differences. Finally, rates of both common illness and serious diseases are higher in developing countries, which places even greater demands on adult caregivers (77–78).

Clearly, a series of reasons explains why many women in parts of the South feel the global crisis of care more strongly. However, there are dangers in drawing this distinction too sharply. Within the industrialized North, there are vast differences in state responses to care—consider the contrast between the social democratic Nordic countries, for example, and liberal economies such as that of the United States (Heymann et al. 2004). Moreover, within individual nation-states, care work is overwhelming undertaken by women of color and of ethnic minorities of low socioeconomic status. Similarly, within many developing countries, the legacy of colonialism maintains the situation whereby domestic and caring work is done for the white minority by poor women of color. Thus, while women the world over face challenges and choices regarding the balancing of work and care, the situation in the Global South illustrates that the politics of caring reveals power inequalities related not only to gender but also to race and locational politics. This situation is often made worse by the effects of violent conflict, environmental disasters, or chronic health crises.

The Global Care Crisis: Consequences and Coping Strategies

> Laura was raising her 18-month-old daughter alone since the death of her husband. She worked in a foreign-owned factory 7 days a week. The shifts were inhumanely long—ranging from 15 to 22 hours a day. But it had been the only job she could find. It was summertime, and Laura's niece temporarily provided care for her daughter, but she was due to return to school in a month. Earning only $26 every 2 weeks and having to pay $14 to the factory for the one meal a day she received, Laura earned too little to afford child care. Soon she would have to choose between trying to get her 10-year-old niece to drop out of school

to provide care—with the inevitable long-term consequences for the life options available to the girl—and leaving her own toddler home alone—as too many others in her neighborhood had been forced to do. (Heymann 2003a: 1)

This is the story of a woman living in the slums surrounding Tegucigalpa, Honduras, as told by Jody Heymann. This short paragraph tells a long and complex story about the gendered consequences and coping strategies of women in the South when faced with their own crises of care. In some developing countries, many adults are forced to work extended hours in order to provide for the needs of their families. A workweek of sixty hours of paid labor outside the home, for all adults in a household, is not uncommon in many developing countries (Heymann, Earle, and Hanchate 2004: 250). This represents a twelve-hour workday—every day of the week—even before transportation is included. This situation has obvious implications for children's and adults' physical and emotional health and safety.

Leaving young children home alone to care for themselves is a common coping strategy in many income-poor countries. In a study done by the Project on Global Working Families, large percentages of respondents in developing countries—50 percent in Botswana, 20 percent in Vietnam—reported that they had left their children home alone. Of those, similarly large percentages—33 percent in Botswana, 29 percent in Vietnam—reported that their children had experienced accidents or other emergencies (Heymann, Fischer, and Engelman 2003: 88). In order to avoid a situation where young children have to stay home alone and unsupervised, parents often turn to their older female children, or their older girls within the extended family, to care for the young children. As a result, these older girls are missing much of their schooling or dropping out completely. Instead of attending school and gaining an education that could enrich their lives and help their employment prospects in the future, these girls are taking on a weighty physical and emotional burden at a very young age.

Another solution to the problem of fulfilling both care work and paid labor responsibilities is to alter the nature and location of income-earning work. Indeed, this double burden, combined with deteriorating work conditions in the formal economy and decreasing state welfare, is putting increasing pressure on families—especially women—to engage in informal activities to compensate for declining resources (Peterson 2003: 87). As Spike Peterson has argued, global restructuring has dramatically increased the volume, value, extent, and sociopolitical significance of informal-sector activities (2003: 85). Informal economic activities are undertaken largely by women, migrants, and the poor. Many women "choose" informal labor because it is often located in the home, so they can carry out their own caretaking and their income-earning work simultaneously. Moreover, it is important to note that gender hierarchies intersect with those of race/ethnicity, class, and national patterns in determining which households engage in which forms of informal labor. While these are related to what types of work are available and where informalization is concentrated, the relationship largely comes down, quite simply, to who is most likely to be available for and willing to undertake informal activities (89).

Mehrangiz Najafizadeh describes how these trends have materialized in post-Soviet Azerbaijan. The closure of Soviet factories, and with it the loss of formal-sector jobs, has led to a dramatic rise in informal-economy activities during the post-Soviet transition. Many women have turned to the informal sector to take on the role of sole or primary breadwinner—especially in situations where husbands have migrated in search of work. This, of course, is in addition to their traditional responsibilities as the main family caregiver. In the economy context of transition, which has included the elimination of state services—including medical, child, and elder care—this dual role for women has been particularly difficult (Najafizadeh 2003: 296).

As Najafizadeh's research has demonstrated, however, Azeri women should not be constructed as the passive and vulnerable victims of these burdens. Since 1991, more than twenty nongovernmental Azeri women's advocacy associations have emerged that bring women's issues to the forefront of public debate and attempt to influence social policy. These associations are now providing particular types of caregiving services (Najafizadeh 2003: 298). Importantly, these associations are engaged in a dual function: to serve as caregivers to women—providing medical and legal assistance, family counseling, or job training; and to assist women in becoming more effective caregivers to their own families and communities through the provision of prenatal, child, and elder care and in teaching skills for income generation (303).

Similarly, in her study of women in Suriname, Mayke Kromhout argues that many women have turned to a variety of sources of alternative income because of the great difficulties they experience in holding on to their jobs in the formal sector. The specific survival strategies these women use demonstrate the importance of caring work in their day-to-day lives and the ways in which household composition is changing to facilitate social reproductive tasks. Many Javanese women in Suriname who are entering the labor market use their extra earnings to provide housing for relatives in return for the sharing of domestic tasks such as child care and food preparation. This strategy of "house sharing" is a way of coping with the obvious difficulties that women experience in combining work for production with the management of their households (Kromhout 2000: 147).

Given the conditions in many developing countries, it is perhaps not surprising that a number of women eschew factory or informal work in favor of state-sponsored domestic worker migration programs. The migration of care workers from the Global South to the Global North is a startling example of a pervasive, yet often hidden, side of globalization. Of course, these patterns of migration are not happening spontaneously: rather, they have been aided by the state-sponsored spread of such solutions in Western Europe, often fueled by a mix of still-hegemonic mother-substitute "ideals of care" and immigration regimes that facilitate such flows (Mahon and Robinson, forthcoming). American researchers have documented the heavy reliance of U.S. families on (documented and undocumented) women migrants from South America and elsewhere (Parreñas 2001; Ehrenreich and Hochschild 2002), whereas in Canada, the Domestic Live-In Caregiver program has attracted a large number of female domestic workers from the Philippines (Bakan and Stasiulis 1997; Tronto, forthcoming).

While there has been some research done on the threats to human security faced by migrant domestic workers—including exploitation because of unregulated home-based employment, physical confinement, and sexual abuse—the relational nature of human security in this context is rarely explored. Women who migrate for domestic labor usually leave children behind. Sometimes they leave behind a husband who is the father of those children; often, the fathers have already left (Parreñas 2001: 85). Thus, they must find care for their children; often, this responsibility falls to an older sibling or relative from the extended family. Migrant women often support dependent relatives beyond the immediate family, thus sustaining "interdependent transnational ties" in migration (84). The global care chain phenomenon demonstrates vividly the relational nature of economic insecurity in the short term and explains how gender, racial, and class norms related to care work perpetuate inequalities within the global economy.

As Barbara Ehrenreich and Arlie Russell Hochschild note, this pattern of female migration reflects not only systemic North-South and gender inequality but also what could be called a "world-wide gender revolution" (2002: 3). As discussed previously, fewer families, in both rich and poor families, rely solely on a male breadwinner for household income. To compound this, the numbers of people requiring sustained or continuous care, for example, infirm, elderly, or disabled adults, has grown (Stasiulis and Bakan 2003: 24). When all adults are working outside the home and the state continues to withdraw from care areas, care for children, the sick, and the elderly must come from somewhere. In the Global South, as previously explained, this care often comes from older siblings or extended family members. In the worst cases, it is simply not provided, and children and other dependents are left to fend for themselves. In the Global North, however, more and more women, who must juggle paid employment with domestic responsibilities, are turning to poorer and more vulnerable populations to help them carry out their obligations in the private sphere while continuing to participate in the public sphere.

While some may choose to see this as a convenient fit between women needing care workers and other women needing jobs, the reality is far more complex. First, this explanation overlooks the role of men, who have, globally, done little to increase their contribution to care work in spite of the increase in paid employment of women. Seen in this way, the presence of immigrant nannies does not enable affluent women to enter the workforce; it enables affluent men to continue avoiding the second shift (Ehrenreich and Hochschild 2002: 9). Second, a simple reading of this phenomenon overlooks the marked failure of most states in the industrialized North to meet the needs created by its women's entry into the workforce, through, for example, public child care or paid care leave (9–10).

Of course, it should go without saying that not all women in the North who work outside the home have chosen, or indeed are able, to employ foreign care workers. Many employ ethnic or racial minority women who are citizens or permanent residents of that particular nation-state; alternatively, they may be illegal immigrants, relied upon for work such as this to support the economy. Moreover, women of color staff most of the institutions providing care, including day cares, preschools, and nursing homes. The intensely gendered and raced nature of care work can be explained partly by economics; care work is undervalued and underpaid and regarded as not requiring "skills"—hence, it perpetuates a cycle of poverty for many women. It is also driven, however, by widespread assumptions that this "kind of work" is suitable for women—in particular, women of color. Thus, the failure of governments in developed countries to respond to the changing nature of women's work has resulted in policies and programs that perpetuate the gendered, raced, and global division of care work.

Sex Work, Security, and Morality

> Sex service discourse is not so different from discourses on housework and caring, all trying to define tasks that can be bought and sold as well as assert a special human touch. Paid activities may include the production of feelings of intimacy and reciprocity, whether the individuals involved intend them or not, and despite the fact that overall structures are patriarchal and unjust. (Agustin 2007: 62)

"Sex trafficking" is often cited as a key example of the "new human security threats" facing vulnerable individuals—especially vulnerable young women—in a globalized world. The dominant discourses of sex trafficking emerge from media and state representations and convey a picture of "victims" as a homogenous, passive group. This is in contrast to the active agents of organized crime who engage in these illegal activities for their own personal economic gain.

Unlike the global care economy, which is widely thought to be morally unproblematic, the global "sex economy" is rife with moral discourse. Interestingly, there is little consensus as to what constitutes the central ethical debates surrounding these practices. This is reflected in the priorities of various anti-sex-trafficking groups, who identify trafficking as a problem for very different reasons and have very different political agendas with regard to the issue (O'Connell Davidson 2006: 7). Thus, for many states, the problem with sex trafficking arises out of issues concerning irregular immigration and transnational organized crime. For human rights NGOs, interest is often based around labor rights and concerns about "modern slavery" (8). For feminist abolitionist groups, often in coalition with groups from the religious Right, prostitution and sex trafficking are condemned as a "social evil" that is asserted to be "immoral" in that it is oppressive and exploitative of women and/or a threat to marriage and the family (Weitzer 2007: 450). It is this group that makes use of the most explicitly "moral" language and that has constructed the fight against prostitution and sex trafficking as a moral crusade. The goals of a moral crusade, furthermore, are twofold, as Weitzer explains: "These movements . . . see their mission as a righteous enterprise whose goals are both symbolic (attempting to redraw or bolster normative boundaries and moral standards) and instrumental (providing relief to victims, punishing evildoers)" (2007: 448). This kind of moral analysis—which relies on the rhetoric of "good" and "evil" and makes authoritative moral prescriptions about threats to the moral and social fabric—fails to incorporate critical moral ethnography, which, I have argued, is a crucial feature of feminist moral inquiry. As Walker argues, it is a central work of feminist moral analysis to analyze the discursive spaces that different moral views (and theories of them) create and to explore the positions of agency and distributions of responsibility that these views foreground or eclipse. Importantly, moreover, it must look at where moral views are "socially sited" and what relations of authority and power hold them in place (M. Walker 1999: 75).

The moral crusades against prostitution and organized crime fail to understand prostitution and sex trafficking in the wider social-moral contexts of the transnationalization of women's sex and care work and the normative structures that uphold those processes. A combination of economic, social, and demographic factors has led to these developments. The broad structural conditions of globalization have led to the growth of "alternative circuits of survival in developing countries." The "growing immiseration" of governments and whole economies in the

South has "promoted and enabled the proliferation of survival and profit-making activities that involve the migration and trafficking of (low-wage and poor) women" (Sassen 2002: 255). In spite of discursive and policy efforts to separate sex workers from other forms of migrant female labor, all of this global women's work may be traced, in large measure, to the same broad norms and processes. As Audrey Macklin argues, there is a global demand for "women's work" that can no longer be supplied by women in affluent, developed states. While the types and nature of this work differ somewhat, all these forms of labor can be made sense of only when viewed through the lens of global gendered relations of power. Thus, as Macklin points out, sex-trade workers supply sex, live-in care-givers perform child care and housework, and so-called mail-order brides furnish all three. Although sex-trade workers are "frequently criminal-ized as prostitutes and 'mail-order brides' are not formally designated as workers (insofar as their labour is unpaid), these migrations occur within a commercialized context where the expectation of economic benefit (to the women and to relatives in the country of origin) structures the incen-tives for entering the process" (Macklin 2003: 464–465).

One solution to the problem of separating sex work from other types of work is to address all of this work from within the framework of women's rights. For example, Christien Van den Anker points to the lack of integration between the discourse on migrant workers' rights and the discourse on women's rights and argues that migrant women "should be an important part of the women's rights agenda" (2006: 180). She insists that, in spite of the fractured and legalistic nature of rights discourse and implementation, a rights approach is regarded as the best way to conceptualize, and potentially to transform, the problem of human trafficking. This is in line with the analytical and norma-tive framework taken by many nonabolitionist feminists toward human trafficking (see Kempadoo 2005; Chang and Kim 2007; Van den Anker 2006), and gender and human security more broadly.

Clearly, rights-based ethics, rights discourse, and human rights law have a role to play in addressing the issue of sex trafficking, in both aca-demic and activist contexts. This is especially the case when rights are seen as embedded in wider structures of globalization and so-called root causes; as Van den Anker argues, "Gender, race, nationality and ethnic-ity are at least some of the factors influencing who ends up trafficked and under which circumstances. Universalist approaches [to rights] therefore need to take into account that these structural and long-term causes may need recognition before equal respect can be implemented" (2006: 179). In this view, rights are not seen as abstract or ahistorical but situated in the gendered effects of globalization and framed by an intersectional approach (179).

However, while this kind of women's rights approach to sex trafficking moves in the right direction—in terms of its commitment to situating trafficking within gendered globalization—it is destined always to see trafficking as a women's rights "issue," and thus of relevance only to women; furthermore, it is likely to remain plagued by debates over universality and difference—especially among so-called first-world and third-world women. Furthermore, a rights-based approach cannot give us insight into *why and how* these abuses are licensed by dominant social and cultural norms or moral understandings. Finally, the methodological and normative individualism of rights-based approaches obscures the relational nature of these processes and the extent to which the moral responsibility to maintain relations of care can provide the basis for a conceptualization of human security in this context.

Understanding the influence of hegemonic norms of masculinity in the constitution of governance rules at global and national levels is crucial to an analysis of the global distribution of both care and sex work. Norms of hegemonic masculinities contribute to the feminizing of domestic, service, and sex work; in so doing, they serve to reify the public-private dichotomy and mute the contradictions of transnational liberalism (Chang and Ling 2000: 41). Just as the articulation of two separate spheres of human social life—the public and the private—served to obfuscate the gender contradictions of early liberal theories of rights, the "transnational ideology of sexualized, racialized service" allows the public, masculine face of globalization to flourish (41).

Kimberly A. Chang and L.H.M. Ling call this public face of violence "techno-muscular capitalism." Techno-muscular capitalism (TMC) is characterized by "Western capitalist masculinity" and "aggressive market competition" in the fields of global finance, production, trade and telecommunications. The other "face" of globalization is the "regime of labour intimacy (RLI)—the explicitly sexualized, racialized and class-based globalization which operates on a symbiotic ideology of racism/

sexism to institutionalize its globalized service economy" (2000: 27, 36). Labor intimacy, Chang and Ling argue, both results from and sustains techno-muscular, "cosmopolitan" globalization (41).

Ironically, constructions of masculinity are also implicated in the contemporary security discourses that seek to "protect" women from "evil" new security threats. From the "war on terror," which sucks immense resources away from caring services, to the hypermoralized responses to the "evildoers" who traffic women across borders, to the justification of militarism in *The Responsibility to Protect*—all these discourses, and the policies that emanate from them, seek to dispel any disruptions to our conventional gender categories and to shift our gaze away from the ways neoliberal globalization, characterized by commodification and massive inequalities, is fatally implicated in all of these so-called security crises, as well as in the more invisible, yet no less threatening, crisis of care.

Notions of masculinity and femininity are necessarily interdependent and intersect with other social relations of power, including race and class. While the language of care may be the "different voice" of women, a critical care ethics eschews gender essentialisms; instead, it seeks to interrogate how and why hegemonic forms of masculinity license men's neglect of caring responsibilities and contribute to the manipulation of images of care and womanhood into images of female subservience and sexual service. By challenging the public-private dichotomy and the naturalization of women's caring and "service" work, a critical ethics of care politicizes these gendered acts and links them to ideologies that denigrate the moral values and activities associated with caring. These values include attentiveness and responsiveness to the needs of others, as well as the development of the patience and trust necessary to sustain long-term commitments to particular persons. The degradation and feminization of care are related not only to the dominance of norms of economic self-sufficiency but also to the social, political, and cultural legitimation of male domination, aggression, and "abusive neglect."

At the global level, both neoliberalism and militarism are characterized by a blindness to interdependence, vulnerability, and the public role for caring practices in creating societies that are less prone to conflict and less reliant on violence as a solution to social problems. As

Colleen O'Manique has argued, we must move beyond a focus on "male domination" toward an examination of a system of extreme masculine characteristics, which are reflected in the valorization and celebration of war and violent masculinity, and the devalorization of the labor of social reproduction more typically performed by women (2006: 174).

It is again important to stress that claims about the construction of hegemonic forms of masculinity are not the same as claims about the behavior of individual men. Indeed, essentialist arguments—about, say, male aggression or female passivity—cannot accommodate the many "variations that exist among both men and women in terms of their attitudes toward, and participation in, acts of violence" (Whitworth 2004: 154). Moreover, to refer to "hegemonic masculinity" is not to deny the existence of multiple visions of masculinity (and femininity) that may coexist; rather, it is to acknowledge the social practices through which one vision may predominate over others to become "culturally exalted" or hegemonic (Connell, quoted in Whitworth 2004: 154). Finally, as a pattern of hegemony in the Gramscian sense, rather than a pattern of simple domination based on force, socially dominant masculinities are maintained by cultural consent, discursive centrality, institutionalization, and the marginalization or delegitimation of alternatives (Connell and Messerschmidt 2005: 846). If we are really concerned about human security, maybe we ought to consider redirecting our attention toward the ways in which these forces are at work today in the global context.

The Ethics of Care, Human Security, and "Women's Work"

The domestic and caring sector is often referred to as feudal, involving servitude and servility. How is it that these social phenomena are looked on so uncritically within Western societies?

—AGUSTIN 2003

Using a critical feminist ethics of care as a moral framework through which to view human insecurity related to transnational care work and sex work shifts attention toward an examination of the wider context in which these activities take place. Rather than regard female care and sex workers, their employers and clients, and their immediate and extended families as autonomous individuals who either possess or lack agency to make moral decisions, a critical ethics of care regards all people as embedded in networks of relationships. Relative power, degrees of agency, and moral responsibilities are mediated through these relationships. Some of these relationships may be nurturing and life sustaining, while others may be exploitative or violent; in all cases, however, it is the relationships that are central to determining the conditions affecting human security and insecurity in this context.

A feminist care ethics approach to human security facilitates a critique of the stereotype of care as "bottomless feminine nurturance and self-sacrifice" (M. Walker 1999: 108). Critics of care ethics—including some feminists—have argued that an ethic of care can serve to reinforce gender stereotypes and can "look like the lamentable internalization of an oppressively servile social role" (108). An ethics of care that is essentialist, uncritical, and "unpoliticized" risks romanticizing the activities of care and of using women's "natural responsibility" to care as a justification for female servitude. That care could be degraded in this way—to legitimize sexual and domestic service and the violence associated with it—however, is a result of the development of particular moral understandings, including hegemonic forms of masculinity, that are mediated through gendered relations of power. As Jan Pettman argues, the domestication of women naturalizes men's sex right to women's bodies, labor, and children. Women are there to service men, providing domestic and sexual labor, which is assumed to be a labor of love (Pettman 1996: 186).

While there is no essential picture of what good caring relations should look like, a critical ethics of care emphasizes the benefits to all people of an image of care that recognizes responsibility and responsiveness to particular others as positive expressions of both masculinity and femininity. Feminist ethics must reclaim the role of caring values as a positive, valuable aspect of all societies and of caring labor as an important practice of contemporary citizenship. In the context of global politics, it asserts that the adequate provision of care, and equitable distribution of responsibilities for care, is a basic prerequisite for human security.

In Chapter 1, I introduce and develop the relationship between hegemonic masculinities, neoliberal globalization, and the feminization of care as an important normative structure contributing to widespread insecurity for people, their families, and communities around the world. Understanding the influence of hegemonic masculinities in the constitution of governance rules at global and national levels is crucial to an analysis of the relationship between "global women's work" and human security. Indeed, this can help explain why these rules have yet to give due recognition to the significance of women's work relative to men's work, and women's security needs relative to men's security needs (Truong 2003: 32). As Thanh-Dam Truong argues, whereas care for people who are old, sick, or young—socially defined as women's work—tends to meet with less supportive responses from state-based and community-based entitlement systems, care for men's sexual needs is highly responsive to market forces (32–33).

Contemporary forms of hegemonic masculinity are constructed through accounts of femininity as caring, docile, dependent, and self-sacrificing. Importantly, these accounts in the context of the sex trade are also raced and thus construct this type of femininity as foreign, exotic, and "Other."[2] Here, relations of gender and race intersect; as Pettman argues, in a postcolonial era, colonial relations live on in racialized power differences and intensifying relations of dominance, subordination, and exploitation (1996: 198). While the language of care may be the "different voice" of women, a critical care ethics must eschew gender essentialisms and interrogate how hegemonic forms of masculinity license are linked to the disassociation of men and masculinity with caring values and activities, and how this contributes to the manipulation of images of care and womanhood into images of female subservience and sexual service.

Toward a New Global Political Economy of Care

Consideration of human security in the context of "women's work" in the global economy—especially domestic, care, and sex work—requires

---

[2] The extent to which race is a useful concept for analysis of trafficking in women is contested. Laura M. Agustin argues that the fastest-growing group of migrants comes from Eastern Europe and the former Soviet Union—women usually considered "white" and "almost" European. Thus, she says, although "exoticizing" may well be taking place, race is not a useful concept for analysis at this time (2003: 378).

engaging in "critical moral ethnography" in order to uncover the moral understandings that license and legitimize the flourishing global care and sex economies. I have suggested that such an approach to ethics requires seeing these moral understandings as embedded in the structures and processes of the gendered global political economy. The prevalence of these forms of labor in the contemporary global economy demonstrates how the values and practices of care have been denigrated and manipulated by unequal power relations of gender and race and by wider inequalities in the global political economy.

The naturalized epistemology of a feminist ethics of care means that there are no obvious normative or policy prescriptions that flow from it. However, it does start with some clear ontological arguments about relationality and the life-sustaining significance of caring relations and caring responsibilities for all human flourishing. It regards these relations and responsibilities as neither simply "natural" nor "contractual" but as fundamentally ethical. As such, they are inseparable from, and indeed constituted by, the social, economic, and political arrangements in which they are embedded in household, local, and global contexts. Furthermore, arrangements for care in particular contexts may be judged "better" or worse"—they may be characterized by inequalities, exploitation, and oppression or by fairness, transparency, trust, and equity. Responsibilities for care may be gendered and raced, or they may be distributed based on the assumption that all persons are bearers of responsibilities to care for others.

Current trends in globalization—specifically, the sexualization and commodification of female migrant labor within peripheral sites and the accelerating exchange of money for bodies—are part of wider trends toward neoliberal restructuring that contribute to the socioeconomic and political conditions that feminize, racialize, denigrate, and undervalue the values and activities of care. Rather than be upheld as a fundamental, life-sustaining activity of citizenship, care is associated with subservience, self-sacrifice, dependence, and a lack of agency. Care work, domestic work, and sex work—increasingly done by migrant women of color—occupy the lowest rungs on the ladder of "success" in the global political economy. Often alone and "out of place," these women are, ironically, highly vulnerable in terms of their lack of relationship networks, family, and formal citizenship status. Thus, these foreign carers are perhaps the least likely to receive good care, and many lead lives that are perpetually insecure.

While changes in policy at the level of state welfare policies and international financial institutions are crucial, some change in local and global notions of masculinity and femininity is necessary if real transformation to the global organization of care, and the nature of "women's work" more generally, is to take place. In her analysis of the global "sex economy," Thanh-Dam Truong argues that cultural means must be found to deal with forms of expression of masculinity that are harmful to the integrity of women and children as social beings. Current expressions of masculinity in the sex trade need to be countered with "images of virility as the ability to care and take responsibility for the other" (Truong 2003: 48). She argues for a notion of "caring and responsible" sex (as distinct from "safe sex") that seeks not only to enhance personal safety but also to promote a cultural transformation toward nonviolence in sexuality. It is through nonviolence, she argues, that mutual respect can be built and a gender-based human security achieved (48).

Attempts to define what sex should "look like," however, are problematic and may lead back to the same "moralizing" debates that continue to dominate the ethical discussion of prostitution and sex trafficking. I would argue, in contrast, for a broader reanalysis of the role of care in societies—both domestically and at the level of global society. This involves understanding the neoliberal and masculinist sleight of hand through which "new geographies of inequality" have simultaneously made care a more pressing concern and marginalized care from view (Lawson 2007: 2). Unlike a women's rights approach, a critical care ethics approach can help us understand *why* women are economically and physically exploited and subject to violence through elucidating the wide connections between femininity and subservience on the one hand, and masculinity and autonomy on the other. Shifts in moral understandings toward the valuing of care and the reshaping of visions of masculinity and femininity must go hand in hand with the recognition of care as the very basis of active citizenship and human security.

4 | Humanitarian Intervention and Global Security Governance

A care ethic provides a substantive basis for applying the ethics of responsibility.

—Tronto, forthcoming

While most of the literature on global governance addresses the rules, norms, and institutions of global economic governance—including trade and finance—a growing body of work explores security and intervention from a governance perspective (see Griffen 2000). What this means is that the interplay of purposive activities and strategies of state and nonstate actors, formal and informal rules and discursive practices, and wider material and ideational structures surrounding security and intervention are recognized as exercising significant forms of authority over communities of people around the world today.

For analytical purposes, recent history with respect to global security may be divided into at least three, and possibly four, time periods. Broadly speaking, the first period—immediately following the end of the Cold War—saw the growth and development of notions of human security, which emphasized the individual as the primary referent of security and broadened the notion of security to include, among other things, the exercise of basic human rights; it also saw the development of new practices and norms regarding humanitarian intervention, which emphasized the global community's "responsibility to protect."[1] It is widely understood that the second time period—directly following September 11, 2001—was characterized by a return to militarized, state-centric conceptions of security, the subordination of individual human rights, and a delegitimation of the norms of humanitarian intervention. While characterizing and framing a third period is difficult, it could be suggested that the second half of the first decade of the twenty-first century was characterized by increased diversity among different state actors regarding the trade-offs between "national" and "human" security. Finally, it is arguable that the global financial and economic crisis that began in 2008 will mark the beginning of a new period, which, for some states, will be characterized by a shift in attention away from the "war on terror" toward the attainment of basic economic security. Notably, in 2009, a report released by the Montreal Centre for Genocide and Human Rights Studies seeks to reinvigorate the principles of R2P, focusing specifically on measures designed to create and foster the "will to intervene" to prevent "mass atrocities" (Will to Intervene 2009). While this report does not advocate a withdrawal from militarized solutions to crisis situations, it does seek to reorient policy attention away from protecting "ourselves" from "our enemies" toward protecting civilians in fragile or failed states (Will to Intervene 2009).

This picture, however, while analytically useful, obscures the subtleties of the ways in which the norms, institutions, and practices of "global security governance" are contested and the complex ways in which they are played out politically. It is necessary to look inside these broad understandings of the trajectories of global security governance in order to understand how they have created and perpetuated hegemonic discourses that have effectively silenced alternatives. In particular, while the human security approach—especially in the context of the United Nations and the independent Commission on Human Security—has made an effort to integrate gender-based inequality and violence, the overwhelming reliance on a universalist human rights framework ignores the potential critical contribution of feminist ethics

---

[1] International Commission on Intervention and State Sovereignty. 2001. Henceforth, *The Responsibility to Protect* will be referred to as R2P.

in conceptualizing the nature of insecurity, not only for women but for all people in the context of families and communities around the world.

With this in mind, I analyze humanitarian intervention through the lens of a critical feminist ethic of care. I argue that conventional accounts of the ethics of global governance suffer from what Cynthia Enloe calls the "underestimation of power"; feminist ethics, by contrast, focuses critical attention on the ways in which normative structures and discursive power serve to sustain existing patterns of gender relations and other forms of inequality; moreover, it relies on a moral ontology that is based on the relationships that inhere within particular "social-moral systems" (M. Walker 1998). Using this understanding of ethics as both a normative and methodological lens, I explore the discourse of R2P in order to expose its limitations as frameworks for security in the twenty-first century. While R2P, which relies heavily on a human security framework, makes a genuine effort to address not only "reacting" but also "preventing" and "rebuilding," it lacks the conceptual and policy tools to actually address the root causes of many humanitarian emergencies. The result is a document that reluctantly but resolutely confirms the need for moral principles that can justify the use of violent solutions to particular, complex, historically rooted, and culturally situated crises.

In spite of its cosmopolitan rhetoric, R2P relies on an "inside/outside" dichotomy that assumes the presence of communitarian loyalties as an obstacle to be overcome (see R. Walker 1992). In so doing, it overlooks many widespread forms of moral and social exclusion—including gender exclusion—that result from the alignment of elite interests around the interests of global capitalism as a feature of contemporary global governance. The central moral ideas and frameworks of these discourses limit both our understandings of the problems that exist and the potential solutions that may be available. The key terms of the R2P discourse—"rights," "autonomy," "responsibility," "protection"—are all understood in the context of a "moment of crisis," and thus they ignore the permanent background to insecurity and humanitarian crises. This background exists before, during, and after the conflict and is played out not by isolated individuals seeking to claim their rights but in relationships of responsibility—in households, refugee camps, factories, hospitals, chronic care facilities, community meetings, schools, and day cares. Attention to the complexity of conflict and postconflict situations, and the role of women and caregiving in those contexts, exposes the inadequate and gendered ethics of the contemporary global governance of security and intervention.

Ethics and Power in Global Governance

While there is widespread consensus that analyses of global governance must pay close attention to norms and the normative, surprisingly little academic study focuses explicitly on the ethics of global governance. One exception is "Ethics and Global Governance: The Primacy of Constitutional Ethics," by Mervyn Frost (2004). In this essay, Frost restates his earlier arguments about international ethics as "constitutive"; this view holds that actors are constituted as such within a range of diverse social practices, all of which have built into them specific sets of values or ethical codes (54–55). In this view, ethical analysis of global governance involves asking whether the ethics underpinning the practices of democratic and democratizing states are compatible with those underpinning global civil society (62). While this question remains open, Frost appears to be optimistic, since he asserts that for both sets of practices, the fundamental values are those associated with the idea of individual autonomy (63).

Earlier in the chapter, Frost repeats another of his arguments about the nature and role of ethics in the study of international relations. He argues that both mainstream and "critical" approaches to the discipline ultimately neglect ethics in their analysis by focusing too heavily on "power" (42). He describes this as "ironic," given that many critical theorists overtly stress the importance of ethics.

A critical feminist approach radically opposes this understanding of the ethics of global governance. First, it rejects the understanding of global governance as a process of the increasing democratization of states around the world. Instead, global governance is seen as encapsulating the "shift from 'state/government' to 'multi-layered' governance, not only of states and markets but also of interstate relations and security" (Rai 2004: 579). While global governance is certainly shaped by struggles of nonstate actors against the consequences of globalization, it is also defined by the discursive and material power of the world's most powerful states, aligned toward the needs of a gendered global capitalist economy (580; see also Cox 1996). This alignment, which has been described as the "politics of convergence," is most visibly manifested in the rules and institutions governing the global capitalist economy; those same rules, however, are integral in governing noneconomic aspects of global governance, including the discourses and politics of human rights, democratization, security, and humanitarian intervention.

With this in mind, feminist approaches to the ethics of global governance also reject the claim that critical IR theory ignores ethics because it focuses too much on power. On the contrary, the focus on power provides the basis for understanding the nature of morality and the methodology for ethical analysis, in critical approaches to ethics, that are concerned with the ways in which moral argument and discourse can serve to support or disrupt existing structures and relations of power. Furthermore, analysis of power relations is necessary not only for critique of existing social-moral systems but also for the development of accounts of their transformation. In other words, understanding the nature of material and discursive power relations is imperative if one is to determine the nature and limits of ethical possibility—how deep-seated moral understandings may be transformed over time to become less exclusive.

Feminist ethics has played a particularly important role in conceptualizing the relationship between morality and different forms of power. It has, as Margaret Walker confirms, provided "unprecedented theoretical understandings on the moral meaning of relations of unequal power." Perhaps most important, the feminist theorization of the morality of *unequal* power has challenged the focus of traditional moral theory on reciprocal exchanges. By contrast, feminist understandings of "power over," "responsibility for," and "dependency on" compel us to "see our moral being in terms of varied relations, both symmetrical and asymmetrical, immediate and highly mediated, to others" (M. Walker 2003: 105). From the perspective of a feminist ethics of care, for example, dependency and vulnerability are incorporated into the concept of a "normal" subject (Sevenhuijsen 1998: 146). Thus, this approach to ethics eschews the tendency in traditional moral theory to shunt to the bottom of the agenda any relationships between those who are clearly unequal in power—including parents and children, large states and small states (Baier 1995: 28). As Annette Baier has argued, a complete moral philosophy would tell us how and why we should act and feel toward others in relationships of shifting and varying power asymmetry and shifting and varying intimacy (120). This kind of moral philosophy, moreover, may be more helpful concerning the design of institutions structuring those relationships between unequals (28).

Furthermore, a feminist ethics of care regards *caring activity* as fundamental to human life. While care is often assumed to involve reciprocal and nonconflictual feelings of "love, empathy and involvement" among equals, empirical research into the lived experiences of those in relations of care demonstrates the need to grapple with the moral questions that arise from conflicting views of needs, as well as the inherent difficulties of situations of dependency, vulnerability, and major differences in the possession of power resources (Sevenhuijsen 1998: 84). Moreover, as Sevenhuijsen points out, the ethics of care must be recognized as a form of *political* ethics; relations of care take place within political contexts, "in situations of communal interaction and collective deliberation and decision making" (147). All societies make political decisions about caring—including who will do it and under what circumstances.

This leads to the other of Frost's arguments that are rejected by feminist ethics—in particular, the sweeping ontological claim that the values of "individual autonomy" are fundamental to global civil society, and the related normative claim that global governance is "ethical" if its values are "compatible" with these. Feminist moral theory poses serious challenges to both the ontological and normative arguments surrounding individual autonomy. The dominant ontology of autonomy—of isolated, self-reliant moral selves—does not adequately reflect social reality in most communities around the world. Feminists have argued that one of the effects of this ontology has been to obscure from view the particular experiences of women, who are most likely to define themselves in and through their relations with children and other family members—including those who are elderly or chronically ill—or with friends or members of their communities. However, the picture of "autonomous man" does not only distort the experiences of women; all people live lives that are, at least during some periods of time, interdependent with those of others. An ethics based solely on an ontology of autonomy will ensure that moral thinking on global governance always remains in the realm of the "ideal" and will not translate well into social reality in many contexts.

But even as an ideal, autonomy is questionable as a primary normative commitment. Although it is deeply embedded in the moral, political, and economic traditions of liberalism, feminists have interrogated the prominence of this gendered value in Western societies. Frost claims that the values of autonomy are "fundamental" to global civil society and democratizing states; to make this claim, however, is to take a narrow, gendered view of the nature and composition of both civil society and democracy and to overlook the way that many people live lives in which the giving and receiving of care play a fundamental part. Indeed, simply to assert that global governance is ethical if it shares the values of autonomy assumes that all those being governed share this value and that it would provide a good moral foundation upon which to make policy to improve their lives.

In contrast to Frost's arguments, I suggest that thinking about the ethics of global governance *must* involve an interrogation of the discursive and material power behind the dominant norms, ideas, and institutions that currently guide and shape our world. As Shirin Rai argues, gendered readings of global governance ask who is being governed, in whose interests, and how; as such, they can provide insights into the definitional exclusions with which we start our explorations of global governance (2004: 592). A feminist ethical approach, furthermore, would concentrate on the way in which gendered power intersects with and is shaped by relations of race and ethnicity, as well as structures of economic, geopolitical, military, and discursive power. It does this in order to determine how and why global governance is upheld by a particular set of rules and norms, and why other values and moral ideas are hidden and denigrated. The feminist moral theorist is not engaged in dictating moral rights and wrongs from a privileged epistemological position; rather, she is committed to critical analysis of how social-moral systems may exclude and oppress certain groups and to an evaluation of when, and under what circumstances, changes to dominant moral values toward greater inclusion may be possible.

Humanitarian Intervention as Global Governance

As I have argued, human security emphasizes a shift from the state to the individual as the primary referent of security; that individual, moreover, is defined only in the cosmopolitan sense as a "human being," possessing fundamental, individual, human rights. T. Dunne and N. Wheeler argue that what is required in order to achieve human security is the "growth of a cosmopolitan moral awareness such that we come to empathize with and respond to the sacrifices made by those fighting for basic rights in repressive regimes" (2004: 19). But it is not at all evident that a cosmopolitan, individualistic ontology can adequately equip moral agents to "empathize with" the particular contexts in which other agents struggle to achieve basic security. Moreover, despite the "critical credentials" of cosmopolitanism in IR theory, I argue that the cosmopolitanism of the liberal human security approach supports the status quo more than challenges it. As Mohammed Nuruzzaman argues, social change through incremental reforms is the principal objective of the human security paradigm. "The human security paradigm, in the name of policy recommendations, attempts to reform the existing system and, like the realist security paradigm, supports the prevailing social order and hence the socially powerful" (2006: 299).

This limited commitment to change is also evident in the 2001 report of the International Commission on Intervention and State Sovereignty (ICISS). While the authors eschew the term "humanitarian intervention," they describe the kind of intervention with which they are concerned as "action taken against a state or its leaders, without its or their consent, for purposes which are claimed to be humanitarian or protective" (ICISS 2001: 13). The report proposes military intervention as a "last resort," justified only when "every non-military option for the prevention or peaceful resolution of the crisis has been explored"; however, its primary goal is to determine the conditions under which military intervention may be accepted as morally, legally, and politically justified. Indeed, the sections on prevention in the report are necessarily vague and general, including, for example, the "promotion of civil society," the establishment of "more favourable trade terms," and even "tackling economic deprivation" (24–26). International support should take the form of "development assistance" and "efforts to provide support for local initiatives to advance good governance, human rights, or the rule of law" (21). No detailed theoretical or policy framework is offered for these transformations other than the general emphasis on the delivery of individual human rights. In particular, the emphasis is on holding states accountable to international human rights norms, instruments, and institutions, such as the International Criminal Court (17).

I argue that unstated but implicit in this report is the *impossibility* of addressing the enormous root causes of conflict and the inevitability and ultimate necessity of military intervention as a form of governance, once "prevention options" have been "exhausted" (ICISS 2001: 21). Thus, in spite of the shedding of the term "humanitarian intervention," the focus of attention in the report easily slides back to the ethical and policy dilemma of when, and under what circumstances, military intervention will be necessary. Rather than represent a paradigm shift, R2P advances a view of humanitarianism that is, ultimately, still highly militarized. Despite the emphasis on the "responsibility to prevent," there is little recognition in the report of the need for innovative theoretical analysis and policy tools that will surely be necessary if lasting, meaningful transformation is to occur. While there may indeed be situations where military intervention may appear unavoidable, we must bear in mind the costs of all kinds of violence for societies. As Iris Marion Young has argued, violence not only harms individuals but makes their lives difficult to carry on as before, largely because of the "escalating spiral" problem of violence, whereby the use of violence tends to escalate beyond the specific intentions its uses have, often because violent acts tend to produce violent responses (2003: 258).

Even if used to promote ideals that can be defended as morally right, violence is always, necessarily, destructive; this is the case even if it is perpetrated by legitimately authorized public officials (Young 2003: 262). Thus, according to Young, "it is incoherent to have a general rule according to which established institutions may routinely engage in violent acts, which can make acts of violence morally acceptable" (26). Instead, each case—each story of suffering—must be analyzed morally on its own terms, with full knowledge of the participants involved, the history of the crisis, and its relationship to wider global structures and processes.

Militarism, writes Cynthia Enloe, is an ideology. Among its core beliefs are the assumptions that armed force is the ultimate resolver of tensions, and that, in times of crisis, those who are feminine need armed protection (2004: 219). Moreover, while militarism, and the violence that is at its core, cannot be associated with an "essential" masculinity, it may be linked to a particular vision of masculinity that became predominant in Western culture during the twentieth century. This "hegemonic" masculinity is not determined by some natural characteristics; rather, it is created by social practices (see Whitworth 2004: 155). Just as Sandra Whitworth has questioned the use of individuals (mostly men) trained to fight wars in order to conduct peace missions, the logic of militarized humanitarianism may be most effectively challenged through the use of gender analysis. This must mean not simply inserting a gender analysis into the existing theories and policies surrounding humanitarian intervention; rather, it must mean transforming existing approaches and practices based on an ethics of intervention "not grounded quite so brutally in a politics of violence and exclusion" (Orford, quoted in Whitworth 2004: 186).

This gender analysis extends to thinking seriously about questions of agency. While much is made of the revised understanding of "agency" in human security and the responsibility to protect, these approaches retain a dichotomized, gendered view of agency. In seeking to identify the agents who will be successful in "delivering basic rights"—what they describe as the "litmus test" for human security—Dunne and Wheeler suggest what they call a "multidimensional" approach to agency, which translates into a focus on both states and "global civil society," where the latter is characterized by organizations such as Oxfam, Amnesty International, Médecins Sans Frontières, and Save the Children (2004: 18–19). Dunne and Wheeler do recognize the dangers of emphasizing global civil society as an emancipatory actor—specifically, the tendency to treat "security have-nots" as distant objects of our "liberal sympathy" (20). Yet at the same time they argue that their approach has "put the *victims* of global politics at the center of our academic inquiry" (20, emphasis added). Similarly, the ICISS report claims that the moral language of the "responsibility to protect" implies an "evaluation of the issues from the point of view of those seeking or needing support" (2001: 19). In so doing, it "refocuses the international searchlight back where it should always be: on the duty to protect communities from mass killing, women from systematic rape and children from starvation" (20).

The use of the term "victims" in Dunne and Wheeler's case for human security constructs a dichotomy between the providers of security, the agents, and the recipients of security, the victims. These victims, moreover, are discursively and normatively constructed as gendered and raced; they are constructed in opposition to the "heroic subjects" of humanitarian interventions, which possess the attributes of hegemonic masculinity—"a white masculinity obsessed with competitive militarism and the protection of universal (read imperial) values" (Orford 2003: 67). Surely a "multidimensional approach to agency" should at least include those who experience existential threats to their security on a day-to-day basis. Surely it should at least allow them to "give voice" to their own experiences of insecurity and the particular contexts of "sexism, racism, classicism and violent nationalism" in which their insecurity is experienced (Stern 2006: 192).

Whereas human security is often understood broadly to include what I call the "permanent background" of economic, environmental, and societal insecurity, the "humanitarian" construction of human security relies on a reductionist conception of the provision of personal security rights at the moment of violent, military conflict. While R2P attempts to foreground prevention and rebuilding as important elements of humanitarianism, the primary problem to be worked out in the report is when, and under what circumstances, military intervention is legitimate and justified.

Of course, no amount of attention to the values and practices of care in societies will eliminate violence altogether. Violent conflict leading to profound humanitarian crises, and even genocide, will continue to occur. For this reason, contemporary international ethics has been justifiably concerned with questions surrounding moral responses to violence and genocide. How should we act when violence breaks out? Indeed, many ethicists remind us that current and undoubtedly future circumstances will repeatedly force us to make decisions regarding the legitimate use of military intervention in such contexts (see Lu 2009).

I strongly argue, however, that no ethical principle or set of principles—cosmopolitan, communitarian, or otherwise—exists that can provide us with an ethical framework that can be applied to all such humanitarian crises. The narrative approach of a critical ethics of care, by contrast, which addresses moral problems as stories with complex histories and characters in relations, is a more promising way to confront the moral challenges of human insecurity and humanitarian crises. A feminist ethic of care reminds us that the tasks of caring do not stop when violence, or even genocide, breaks out. On the contrary, while our ability to carry out these tasks may be severely compromised, they become even more urgent under such extreme circumstances. Even while life is being obliterated on a massive scale, life remains. More and more people are left injured and hurt, or without care. Relationships are severed as people die, are severely injured, or are physically displaced by violence. An ethics of care offers no prescription for determining when humanitarian intervention is required. However, it reminds other states and the "international community," as outsiders to conflicts, of the need to scrutinize and pay careful attention to the need for care in war-torn societies and to employ the means necessary to help ensure that adequate care is received. In the long term, the prioritization of care both within societies and at the international level will go some way toward ensuring that a reduction of violence occurs at all levels and that peace, once achieved, may be lasting.

Autonomy, Dependence, and Power

In their revealing and insightful genealogy of "dependency" in the U.S. welfare state, Nancy Fraser and Linda Gordon demonstrate how the discourse of dependency affects not only the social politics of "welfare" in that country but how it maps onto a "whole series of hierarchical oppositions" that define contemporary culture:

> Fear of dependency . . . posits an ideal, independent personality in contrast to which those considered dependent are deviant. This contrast bears traces of a sexual division of labor that assigns men primary responsibility as providers or breadwinners and women primary responsibility as caretakers and nurturers and then treats the derivative personality patterns as fundamental. . . . In this way, the opposition between the independent personality

and the dependent personality maps onto a whole series of hierarchical oppositions and dichotomies that are central in modern
culture: masculine/feminine, public/private, work/care, success/
love, individual/community, economy/family, and competitive/
self-sacrificing. (1994: 332)

They argue convincingly for the need to question our received valua-
tions and definitions of dependence and independence in order to allow
new, emancipatory social visions to emerge (332).

Despite its central place in the construction and constitution of
world politics, the notion of "dependence" has not received much
attention in international theory. Juridically speaking, dependence is
regarded as a relic of the past—something that ceased to exist with the
demise of colonialism following the Second World War. "Dependency"
theory—that version of neo-Marxism that regards "underdevelopment"
in the periphery as the inevitable and ongoing result of "development"
in the core—is regarded in international relations as a theory of "development," and thus as not only outdated but largely outside its disciplin-
ary boundaries. Of course, postcolonial and decolonial theorists have
argued convincingly that forms of economic and cultural neocolonialism govern the relations between the Global North and the Global
South in spite of the end of formal systems of imperialism. Despite their
potentially enormous contribution to our understanding of contemporary world politics, these approaches have yet to permeate the mainstream of both IR theory and international political theory.

The task of redefining the nature of, and relationship between,
autonomy and dependence has been a central theoretical task of most
feminist care ethicists. As Eva Kittay has argued, "as long as we continue to occlude the existence of dependency, our political theory
excludes . . . those who are temporarily or permanently dependent
and are so inevitably . . . those whose labour is devoted to the care of
dependents . . . and the moral social and political importance of relationships of dependency rooted in the facts of human vulnerability and
frailty" (2001: 529). While refocusing our attention in these directions
is an important antidote to liberal theory, it is also crucial that we keep
in view the agency of those who are dependent and the ways in which
various forms of dependency are socially constructed by existing norms,

institutions, and structures. Indeed, it may be that the lenses of postcolonial theory have important contributions to make to an international political theory of care, especially in the context of human security and humanitarianism. For example, while the government and people of Haiti may be temporarily and inevitably dependent on donor countries, especially after the recent earthquake, this fact should not blind us to the agency of Haitians not only in responding to the "crisis" but also in their everyday struggles with poverty. Moreover, the ongoing engagement of the international community with Haiti should reflect not just benevolence but a recognition of the common history of colonialism, slavery, occupation, and "development"—a history that is shared by most states. Placing existing relationships in a wider and longer historical perspective also reminds us that relations of dependence are subject to constant change. Seen in this way, our responsibilities to help alleviate poverty and deprivation arise not out of charity or even contemporary obligations of "development" or "cosmopolitan justice" but out of a common history and an interdependent future (F. Robinson 2010: 138–139).

At the international level, an ethics of care must not be seen to translate simply into benevolent and humanitarian practices through which the strong states and organizations that make up the international community "care for" weaker, vulnerable populations. While I eschew a strongly normative care ethics, the critical potential of the ethics of care goes beyond the ontological arguments about relationality. Also crucial to care ethics is the argument that practices of care are the basic substance of morality. Thus, recognition of responsibilities to particular others and an understanding of the nature of those responsibilities are just the first steps. The next steps involve sustained attention to people not as autonomous rights-bearers but as relational subjects who are both givers and receivers of care.

These ideas may be applied to our moral understandings of contemporary humanitarian situations. In the light of the recent earthquake, "Haiti" is constructed as a vulnerable population in need of benevolence and care. But a critical ethics of care reveals the moral and practical complexity of care in this context. A critical ethics of care asks, "What are the care needs in this context?" and "How are these needs being met?" Answering these questions requires attention not just to the most basic, immediate care needs of those in grave physical condition—the needs of "bare life"—but also to the wider landscape of care in this context. It calls for thinking about how relationships and communities that previously attended to care have been dismantled by events, and what can be done to repair or rebuild those relations, or to find alternative means of providing care. It involves consideration of the distribution of the material, physical, and emotional burdens of care and how these are affected by constructions of gender and race. While recognizing that the negotiation of care provision is fundamentally political, it does not shrink from an explicit consideration of power relations in this context. Contrary to widespread perceptions, rights and interests are important aspects of a critical ethics of care. Rights are crucial in the context of both giving and receiving of care; however, they must always be understood relationally and always as embedded in and realized through existing social and political arrangements. Considering the complex landscape of relations and responsibilities of care in this way is not a short-term process; rather, it is an ongoing task of practical ethics that must always be cognizant of the past, the present, and the short- and long-term future.

The aim of this line of argument is not simply to turn the autonomy-dependency dichotomy on its head; on the contrary, it is to demonstrate that the nature and extent of dependence and interdependence in social, political, and economic life are constantly shifting and evolving, with different kinds of costs and benefits for different actors. Increasingly, the relationships between dependence and power in global politics are not always clear. As previously illustrated, while income-rich states, and individual families within those states, may be dependent upon migrant women to fill the gaps in care provision in their countries, the migrant women themselves are rarely empowered by this relationship. To say this is not to underestimate the agency of these women or the sacrifices they make to provide for their children. Yet as agents they still remain embedded in a wider, structural inequality in which gendered, racialized care work is globally undervalued.

Shades of dependence and interdependence, moreover, are never simple or limited to a single sphere or scale. The lens of a critical ethics of care allows us to see how apparently simple dependence is in fact constituted by and mediated through a range of structural and normative conditions—in the context of households, communities, and the global political economy. An ethics of care that is not attuned to power relations—to the ways in which power operates through discourses and practices of care—runs the risk of reproducing these dichotomies. A critical ethics of care, however, destabilizes the dichotomy between a benevolent, autonomous Global North and a dependent Global South. As Mark Duffield has argued in his analysis of development and security, there is an urgent need to move away from the view of development as a "one-way process between the provider and beneficiary." This, he argues, is a process that emphasizes differences in power and distance, with providers in places of safety, and beneficiaries in zones of crisis (2007: 233). A critical ethics of care "focuses on interdependence and coexistence and the limits to these and makes apparent the potential connections and disconnections between responsibility, care and power, at a variety of scales" (Raghuram, Madge, and Noxolo 2009: 10).

As I have emphasized, concentrating on ways in which to facilitate care among a variety of actors within and across borders is not the same thing as valorizing a caring morality or arguing for its superiority relative to the morality of rights or justice. Rather, it is about using the alternative ontological lenses of interdependence and relationality to reveal the extent to which the practices of care and responsibility, and the moral negotiation and deliberation that surround them, play an important role not only in the day-to-day lives of families and communities but also in the workings of collective actors, including states in the international system. This exercise also reveals the material and discursive bases upon which decisions about responsibilities for care are reached and invites a critical inquiry into the ideational norms and political economy of gender and race that govern care (F. Robinson 2010: 140–141).

The Permanent Background to Humanitarian Crises

As I have argued previously, a feminist analysis of the ethics of human security reveals the privileging of masculinized, individualist/universal ontological assumptions of traditional ethical approaches to global governance. Moreover, in spite of their explicit reference to nonmilitary security threats and responses to humanitarian crises, the inevitability of violence remains inescapable in the R2P discourse. This, in turn, entails the continued pouring of our moral and political energies into the "moment of decision," while hoping that attending to human rights will be sufficient to achieve human security in the longer term.

In the light of this regrounding of human security, feminist ethics may also provide an important alternative lens through which to view the ethics of humanitarian intervention. In 2002, Neta Crawford suggested that an ethic of care might "help us sort out exactly when and how to intervene to help others in a way that is welcome and not idiosyncratic" (429). Specifically, she suggests that an ethic of care could help promote an attitude that "arrests the potential paternalism in the discourse and practice of humanitarian intervention" (430). She reiterates this idea in her 2005 contribution to a "Roundtable on Humanitarian Intervention," claiming that an ethic of care may be a good starting point for thinking about how to discharge our cosmopolitan responsibilities with both "alacrity and respect" (Farer et al. 2005: 233). These suggestions point to an important way in which care ethics may provide a valuable resource for understanding our ethical relations with distant others. The assumption, however, that care ethics necessarily avoids or "arrests" paternalistic tendencies, particularly in humanitarian or peacebuilding contexts, demands further attention and will be taken up in detail later.

The relational ontology of care ethics—which emphasizes human interdependence and mutual vulnerability—overcomes the dichotomies between the "needy" and the "strong," "victims" and "agents," "objects" and "subjects" in the construction of categories in humanitarian intervention. Combined with the revised view of "security" described earlier, this approach also destabilizes the "inside/outside" dichotomy by pushing theorists and policy makers to look at the state of care within their own societies. Finally, it breaks down the distinction between "crisis" and "normality," putting the very idea of "humanitarian intervention" in question.

Thus, from this perspective, crises requiring responses are not limited to ethnic or tribal conflicts within failed or failing states but may exist in normal times within the borders of powerful states. The crisis of Hurricane Katrina is illustrative here. The actual physical crisis of Katrina and its effects required intervention from the state; the indecision, reluctance, and lack of will demonstrated by the Bush administration in responding to this crisis parallels that of powerful Western states when faced with situations like that of Rwanda in 1994 and Darfur today. This calls into question the assumption that the reluctance to act is based on a realist, statist, or communitarian morality that is disinclined to extend the scope of its moral obligations beyond its own borders. Rather, it suggests, by contrast, that what is at work is a powerful alignment of elite interests toward the needs of a gendered, global capitalist economy; this alignment is just as happy to ignore systemic gender oppression, poverty, and human suffering in the United States as it is in the Sudan. Katrina laid bare for the world to see the shocking poverty, inequality, and racial and gender divisions that characterized—in normal times—parts of the city of New Orleans.

A moral framework of critical care ethics would transcend the statist, militarized, gendered discourse of humanitarian intervention and would push theorists and policy makers to address the state of care in *normal times* both within Western liberal democracies and in states in the Global South. Thus, greater attention would be focused on the permanent background to identified "humanitarian crises" in order to better understand how gender relations, as well as those based on religion, ethnicity "culture," race, and class, affect the real, day-to-day lives and security of people, their families, and their communities. A narrative, rather than a principled approach to moral judgment, would demand attention is paid to the particularities of different humanitarian emergencies, including the relationship between the situations and wider social, economic, and geopolitical relations and processes. Humanitarian crises, then, would not be seen as isolated situations that could be characterized either as political (war or other violent conflict) or economic (famine or other kinds of acute material deprivation). Indeed, violent conflicts and their effects would have to be seen within the wider, ongoing context of neoliberal economic restructuring in order to more clearly understand their effects on the security of people, especially, not exclusively, on women and their families. Addressing the nature and distribution of care work in particular contexts allows us to see care not as a "women's issue" but as the political manifestation of our moral responsibilities toward our shared well-being and security. This includes understanding how, and under what circumstances, the burden of care work is increased, how relations of power determine how responsibilities for that burden are assigned, and how mobilizing around care can disrupt the totalizing logics of both patriarchy and capitalism.

5 | Peacebuilding and Paternalism

Reading Care through Postcolonialism

This chapter considers the implications of a feminist ethics of care in the context of peacekeeping and peacebuilding. Three aspects of care ethics are of particular relevance to peacebuilding. First is the recognition and acceptance of dependence and vulnerability in a variety of social contexts, and the specific moral and political responsibilities that flow from this. Violent conflict usually leaves at least some social groupings and their members hurt, broken, and vulnerable. There is a need to accept and understand these vulnerabilities and pay attention to the care needs arising from them. The second aspect, the ontological focus of care ethics on relationality, allows for the possibility of seeing difference and disagreement as neither intractably oppositional nor as something to be overcome through assimilation. Because difference is seen as constructed through relations that are constantly shifting, difference is not necessarily an obstacle to progress but potentially productive of new identities and patterns of responsibility. In this way, the recognition of difference as relationality may be seen as fundamental to the creation of a politics of reconciliation. Third, because care ethics stresses the importance of engaging in long-term relations that seek to solve problems and meet needs, it provides a more durable moral framework for the building of peace, which can never be a short-term enterprise. As Iris Murdoch reminds us, morality is not just about action; it can also be about learning how to wait, be patient, trust, and listen (1997: 159, 357–358). The ethics of care provides the basis for an approach to peacebuilding that rejects the idea of state liberalization as a fast track to peace; rather, care ethics displays a commitment to a slow process of listening to needs, building trust, and rebuilding relations and institutions for the long-term well-being of societies.

Furthermore, in more practical terms, peacebuilding demands sustained attention to the specific care requirements of all those societies affected by war. While I do not suggest that care can act as a normative guide to the behavior of the "victors" toward the "vanquished," I do argue that consideration of the ethics of postwar situations demands attentiveness to the ways in which conflict has affected the quality and availability of care and the distribution of care work, as well as a commitment to collaborative efforts aimed at finding solutions to the adequate and comprehensive provision of care.

Considering care ethics as an approach to peacebuilding, however, is fraught with potential dangers; indeed, this particular context brings to the fore one of the most powerful critiques of care ethics. This argument, articulated most famously by Uma Narayan (1995), is that "paternalistic care" was an important part of the discourse of colonialism and that contemporary care discourses risk reinforcing, rather than challenging, existing relations of power, especially those inscribed by race, culture, and geopolitics. This is a potentially fatal blow for a global ethic of care, especially as a framework for human security, and in the context of peacebuilding in particular. While there are important differences among actors regarding the specifics of its conceptualization and operationalization, peacebuilding is broadly defined as "external interventions that are designed to prevent the eruption or return of armed conflict" (M. Barnett et al. 2007: 36). The language of peacebuilding usually suggests the "neutrality" of external actors, but experience shows that these interventions are most often driven by a particular political agenda.

A "fully feminist" ethics of care can avoid the dangers of paternalism in care ethics. A fully feminist ethics of care means three things. First, we cannot essentialize women's roles as caregivers; rather, we must interrogate the norms and structures that construct care as "feminine."

Attention to relations and practices of care that have become broken, exploitative, or inadequate because of conflict become the focus for building an inclusive, lasting peace.

Second, a fully feminist ethics of care must be democratic. As Joan Tronto has argued, only a society in which all voices can be heard can put in place the requirements of an ethic of care. Specifically, she suggests that a democratic ethic of care requires a substantive focus on the allocation of responsibilities that includes all of the parties in the discussion. Thus, *democratic politics should center upon assigning responsibility for care* (Tronto, forthcoming). Of course, inclusive participatory or deliberative democracy is not an easy thing to achieve in societies. But the recognition that responsibilities for care require full and open participation is the first step toward the achievement of this democracy. Moreover, Tronto's vision is of great importance in that it outlines not only the *procedures* but also the *substance* of deliberation. This understanding of democracy is of particular importance in the context of the challenge of rebuilding, for the long-term, societies torn apart by conflict.

Third, and central to my argument in this chapter, a fully feminist ethics of care must be attuned to historical and contemporary relations of colonialism and neocolonialism. Thus, international actors must not regard themselves as external to local conflicts but must understand such conflicts as historically linked to previous patterns of interdependence, including prior relations of domination and dependency, in which they are implicated. Recognition of the impact of relations of colonialism on patterns of conflict in existing societies is one of the first steps toward an approach to peacebuilding that prioritizes care but eschews paternalism. Through an examination of the ethics of preventing conflict and building peace, I demonstrate how and why a consideration of our shared history of colonial encounter can and must underpin discussions on responsibilities and practices of care in the global context. Seen in this light, care ethics cannot articulate a normative theory of global justice in the traditional sense; instead, it offers an alternative understanding about the substance of morality and provides critical tools for exploring how moral relations are constructed in global politics.

This chapter situates Narayan's critique in the context of the central development in global governance since the end of the Cold War—the rise of "liberal internationalism." While a number of theorists have critiqued the post–Cold War project of governing the "international" through humanitarianism, "preventative" warfare, "state building," and other interventionist practices, most such critiques have concentrated on the assimilative project of liberal cosmopolitanism and modernist discourses of "development" (see Jabri 2007; Duffield 2007; Jaeger 2007). However, very little work reads the practices of liberal internationalism through the lens of care ethics. As a result, the dangers described in Narayan's work have gone more or less unnoticed.

In recent years, a number of scholars—notably in the fields of critical and human geography—have directly linked the ethics of care with the political discourses of a postcolonial world (Sarvasy and Longo 2004; Raghuram, Madge, and Noxolo 2009). While such accounts are often very different from one another, all are notable for their recognition that our contemporary understandings of care in the global context are deeply tied to a colonial past and to a postcolonial present. This is important for the theoretical development of care ethics; it is especially crucial, moreover, to the application of care ethics to questions of global justice. If it is to be argued that practices and policies aimed at global justice must include responsiveness to the needs and care requirements in the global context, then there must be a way of ensuring that this engagement recognizes relationality and dependence while avoiding the dangers of paternalism and "cultural imperialism." Indeed, what is required is positive engagement with the discursive and material aspects of colonialism, race, and gender, as they are intertwined with both historical and contemporary politics of care.

Although care ethics runs the danger of being read as a license for paternalism, there are indications that many of the ideas central to a feminist ethics of care do, in fact, resonate with other approaches to ethics originating outside the West. Research into global feminisms and global moral understandings reveal the convergences and continuities between a critical ethics of care and many understandings of feminism and ethics originating outside Western Europe and North America. This is not to suggest that the ethics of care is universally understood and accepted, nor that it may be molded into a kind of global ethics. On the contrary, given its emphasis on particularity, context, and narrative, this kind of universalizing move would be untenable. However, it does suggest that a critical ethics of care might open up space for dialogue and shared understandings—in ways that liberal and rights-based ethics have not—in the quest to construct a widely accepted ethical basis for global justice.

I first explore the ethics of humanitarian intervention, peacebuilding, and peacekeeping, with particular emphasis on the contributions of feminist ethics, including the ethics of care. I consult the work of, among others, Joan Tronto and Elisabeth Porter, both of whom argue, in different ways, that the ethics of care is an overlooked but crucial framework in the context of preventing conflict and security peace. Then I address the theoretical critiques of care as "paternalistic" insofar as it embodies the ethic of benevolence toward inferior "others" that characterized colonial encounters. In response to these critiques, I explore the points of overlap and connection between a critical feminist ethics of care and several non-Western ethical and feminist ideas, as well as the implications of viewing care through a "postcolonial frame" (Raghuram, Madge, and Noxolo 2009: 6). The insights here will be used to build an argument for a critical ethics of care as a transnational ethical framework for guiding approaches to keeping and building peace.

Ethics and the Politics of Conflict and Peace

The literature on peace, peacekeeping, and more recently, peacebuilding in international relations is extensive and diverse. Broadly speaking, all of this literature refers, in one way or another, to the period following a violent conflict. Some authors are explicit about this and see the line as being distinct; as Roland Paris argues, "Peacebuilding is action undertaken at the end of a civil conflict to consolidate peace and prevent a recurrence of fighting." He continues: "Peacebuilding begins when the fighting has stopped. It is, by definition, a post-conflict enterprise" (2004: 38–39). This is distinct from peacekeeping, which he describes as a primarily military activity that typically concentrates on cease-fire monitoring (38). While the UN peacebuilding architecture focuses on formal approaches to postconflict reconstruction, including institution building and structural reconstruction, many scholars argue for an informal, long-term approach to peacebuilding that addresses the underlying substantive root causes of conflict (Porter 2007: 26).

In recent years, there has been increasing recognition of the vital role played by women in peacebuilding. The landmark Security Council Resolution 1325, adopted in October 2000, acknowledges the importance of involving women in both formal and informal aspects of peacebuilding. There is a growing realization that in recognizing women's tendencies to prioritize issues of education, health, and child care, we are not necessarily essentializing the feminine or confining women to "feminized" roles; rather, women's peace groups regard these concerns as central to the creation of conditions through which peace is meaningful (Porter 2007: 39, 41).

Recently, a number of feminists have argued that feminist ethics incorporates various evaluative tools for examining the means and ends of postwar practice and conduct (Ben-Porath 2008: 65). Elisabeth Porter's 2007 book, *Peacebuilding*, is a major contribution to this literature, providing a comprehensive theoretical account of women and feminist ethics in the context of "real-world" policy and practice surrounding postconflict reconstruction and peacebuilding. Porter draws on feminist ethics of justice and care in order to challenge the gendered dualisms that currently permeate ideas and practices of peacebuilding. Feminist moral and political theory provides the framework for her examination of the positive role played by women in peacekeeping in a variety of contexts. Thus, her work has two goals: to develop a feminist conceptual articulation of peacekeeping and to highlight women's agency as peacebuilders (6). While there is an important role for care ethics in her work, Porter strongly defends the need to "synthesize" care and justice perspectives in order to overcome the harm of polarization. She follows others, including Carol Gould, in arguing that justice and care must exist within a "dialogical interplay" (Porter 1991: 50); thus, justice is not possible without care, and care without justice is oppressive (Porter 2007: 58). The idea of care as "oppressive" suggests the danger of paternalism—where care is overbearing, it can smother agency and construct the recipients of care as weak and vulnerable.

Other feminist theorists have relied more fully on care ethics in order to make specific arguments about the nature of peacebuilding. For example, Joan Tronto has argued that peacekeeping and peacebuilding can be understood as "care practices" (2008: 188). Specifically, she argues that the shift from the "right to intervene" to the "responsibility to protect"—as articulated in the 2001 report of the ICISS discussed previously—represents a paradigm shift from the ethics of justice toward an ethics of care (2008: 182). Cognizant of the argument that R2P might be used by states to rationalize the ongoing liberal justifications of intervention, Tronto argues that the idea of "responsibility to protect" must be developed and refined in a feminist direction. Notably, however, she suggests using the language of "care" rather than the more familiar language of "gender" to avoid a reliance on essentialized notions of gender, and to undercut "self-serving and ultimately damaging appeals to 'gender' on the part of liberal states" (189). Tronto maps out a "care analysis" of humanitarian intervention, which includes the need for attentiveness, responsibility, competence, and responsiveness. Ultimately, she argues that the greatest failing of R2P is that "it did not go far enough" in revising the notion of sovereignty and emphasizing prevention (195–196).

Building on these ideas, Sigal Ben-Porath has suggested that while Tronto's work on care ethics and peacekeeping can inform an extended "jus post bellum" component of just war theory, her approach needs to be amended for this purpose by way of weakening its aim of ending dependence (2008: 62). Instead, Ben-Porath argues that dependence, as distinct from helplessness, should be structured as "an acceptable part of international relations." She insists that Tronto's political ethics of care suggests the possibility of international dependence "that is not colonial, oppressive or exploitative, but rather supportive and mutually beneficial to the states and citizens involved" (66–67).

Ben-Porath's argument leads us in the direction of a fundamental shift in our thinking about international relations. While we may criticize *The Responsibility to Protect* for affirming and even strengthening existing relationships of dominance among states, we must also recognize the impetus for writing that document in the first place. It is clear that the ways in which sovereignty is widely understood have changed since the end of the Cold War; the idea of articulating sovereignty as responsibility grew out of a recognition of this change, as well as the many failed attempts at "humanitarian intervention" since 1989. While those failures may be linked to a number of causes, I suggest that the overall failure to think clearly about sovereignty and intervention arises from our current inability to imagine the relationships between states in any way other than as either relations of mutual autonomy/sovereignty or as unequal relations of dependence and domination—in other words, the negation of sovereignty.

The implication of Ben-Porath's idea is that dependence is a natural feature of long-term social and political relations, and that the nature, degree, and direction of dependencies may shift over time. Importantly, however, she is suggesting that dependence need not be something to be avoided, but that, if understood and practiced properly, relations of dependence, once recognized and accepted, could be mutually beneficial. It also, however, brings to the fore a great danger in care ethics—a danger that has also been posed, in somewhat different language, in the context of humanitarian intervention and peacekeeping: Taking responsibility for those who are constructed as "dependent" may be seen as an act of complicity with colonialism. As Parvati Raghuram, Clare Madge, and Pat Noxolo argue, to posit responsibility in a finite future is to (re)colonize responsibility (2009: 10). Before attempting to address this challenge, however, I return to Narayan's argument, in order to think more carefully about the particular dangers of care ethics in this context and how they relate to the contemporary international context, and to peacebuilding in particular.

Paternalistic Care?

In an important 1995 article, Uma Narayan argues convincingly that "paternalistic caring," of the sort found in colonial discourse, can be wielded as a form of control and domination by the powerful and privileged (135). She draws attention to the ways in which the colonizing project was seen as being "in the interests of, for the good of, and as promoting the welfare of the colonized"—notions that draw our attention to the existence of a colonialist care discourse whose terms have some resonance with those of some contemporary strands of the ethic of care (133–134). Thus, she suggests that the focus on independent, separate, and mutually disinterested individuals—so roundly criticized by feminists—was only part of the liberal story. The other, often overlooked part of that story was that these same subjects had paternalistic obligations and responsibilities to "inferior Others," whether women in their own families or distant colonial peoples (135). Thus, Narayan argues that many aspects of the self-perceptions of the colonizers, in contrast to the traditional picture of liberalism, seem to have depended heavily on their relationship to the colonized:

> This suggests that strands in contemporary care discourse that stress that we are all essentially interdependent and in relationship, while important, do not go far enough if they fail to worry about the accounts that are given of these interdependencies and relationships. . . . While aspects of care discourse have the potential virtue of calling attention to vulnerabilities that mark relationships between differently situated persons, care discourse also runs the risk of being used to ideological ends where these "differences" are defined in self-serving ways by the dominant and powerful. (136)

This kind of critique is of obvious relevance in the context of human security and the theories and practices of peacebuilding in particular. Critics of contemporary peacekeeping discourses and practices have described them as "imperialism's new disguise" (Schellhaas and Seegers 2009) and "mission civilisatrice" (Paris 2002; see also Ayoob 2004; Chandler 2005; Liden 2009). Notably, most of these authors are critical of the deployment of the so-called liberal peace, which is structured by a series of binary oppositions: liberal-illiberal, peace-war, modern-traditional, civilized-barbaric (Liden 2009: 4). Critics also note that a key aspect of the liberal peace is found in the promotion of a form of economic control and regulation to establish market correctives in societies that have been resistant to conventional marketization imperatives (Pugh 2005: 24).

What is striking is the virtual silence within this critical peacebuilding literature on the ways in which discourses of care and responsibility have been positioned within, rather than in contrast to, the liberal peace. Narayan's critique is a potentially fatal blow to feminists who would argue for an ethics of care as an alternative to liberal approaches to peacebuilding. For example, Tronto suggests that "peacekeeping as care" provides a way to answer the objection that the "responsibility to protect" is just another way for "neoliberals to pretend to do good in the world when in fact they only benefit themselves" (2008: 193). If care can realistically be seen to be an integral part of the liberal peace as a neoimperialist project, however, then this answer has no purchase. This is not to say that theorists of care have been uniformly unaware of the paternalistic, and even neocolonial, potential in care ethics. Almost a decade after Narayan's article was published, Wendy Sarvasy and Patrizia Longo took up the challenges posed in Narayan's work in order to demonstrate how feminized neocolonial relations of care are reshaping the practice of world citizenship (2004: 395). Building upon, yet critiquing, a Kantian notion of cosmopolitan citizenship, the authors argue that the transnationalization of care reveals how rights are "actualized and altered in the context of relationships," including relationships between and within states, between employers and domestic workers, within transnational families, between citizens and noncitizens, and within institutions of global governance. Analyzing these relationships allows the authors to develop a new notion of "multilayered citizenship," which challenges the dichotomies of "public" and "private," "the state" and "the global" that characterize standard citizenship discourse (408). Importantly, Sarvasy and Longo suggest that the issue of the transnationalization of care work has implications for the question of the links between care ethics and global politics. Specifically, they suggest that a feminist global politics of care may provide an important critique to the feminized neocolonialism that characterizes the contemporary global political economy (409).

What is innovative about this article is its recognition that Immanuel Kant's anticolonial project cannot be unproblematically applied to the "current feminized neo-colonial context," especially since, in the case of globalized care work, the colonizer is not the visitor but the host (408). In this sense, their expanded and revised notion of world citizenship reveals the global political implications of household relations and "incorporates migrant domestic workers into the project of building and practicing peace" in their capacity as world citizens (407). This kind of argument is important because it demonstrates how the arrows of colonial "care" have, in one important respect, been reversed as a result of the globalization of care work. That said, employers of migrant care workers may still be paternalistic in their attitudes and behavior— even attitudes and behavior that are ostensibly "caring"—toward their employees.

In essence, Sarvasy and Longo's work is not an attempt to rethink care ethics to address the dangers of paternalism and neocolonialism; rather, it is an attempt to transform the basis of citizenship and the nature of rights in the light of feminized, neocolonial relations of care. Thus, while it demonstrates effectively how contemporary resolutions of the need for care have important ethical implications, it does not directly offer a solution to the problems of paternalism in the globalization of care ethics, either within or beyond the context of peacekeeping.

In contrast, recent work from political geography seeks to consider care through the prism of postcolonialism. Writing from within the frame of "ethical geography," Raghuram, Madge, and Noxolo argue that the accepted temporal and spatial frames in which responsibility and care are usually imagined may be extended by routing them through the "imperatives of a postcolonial world" (2009: 5). Because their analysis is embedded in the geographical literature, the authors are particularly interested in how care is stretched across space in different ways and in the spatial (re)arrangements involved in caregiving and care receiving (6). Notably, they argue that much of the literature on care and care work still posits care as a normative "good," often ignoring the asymmetrical orientation toward the other and the hierarchical nature of many caring relationships (7). As an antidote to this, the authors prescribe routing care theory through the "critical terrain of postcolonialism," where interdependency is "not cozy but is seen as contested, complicated and productively unsettling" (10–11).

This argument points in the direction of a radical rethinking of the ethics of care—a direction that may be crucial if it is to carry critical weight in deliberations about the theory and practice of human security in general and peacebuilding in particular. One of the most important insights of care ethics is found in its relational ontology—its claim that subjectivity is constructed relationally and that the substance of morality is to be found in the practices of responsibility that emerge from within these relations. Importantly, however, I argue that the relations that define us are neither natural nor prefigured; rather, they are constructed through the wider structures and institutions—such as the social relations of capitalism, patriarchy, and citizenship—that govern the contemporary world order. While the need for care for all human beings is evident, it is crucial that we remain cognizant of the ways in which structures and institutions, and the forms of power that flow through them, are not only constructive of, but indeed are productive of, the particular ways in which we understand "our" need for care (as opposed to the care needs of others), how those needs should be met, and by whom, and on what terms. Thus, while a critical ethics of care may be tentatively and cautiously prescriptive regarding the importance of foregrounding a *consideration* of care needs—in the context, for example, of security, global health and ecology, and peacebuilding— what it cannot do is prescribe what that care should look like in the service of achieving security.

In order to help ensure, however, that care needs are considered in ways that avoid paternalism and neocolonialism, it is crucial not only to emphasize the "intimacies and generosities" associated with care practices but also to expose the "pain and absences that underpin global relationships touched by histories of (post)colonialisation, exploitation and inequality" (Raghuram, Madge, and Noxolo 2009: 6). As Raghuram and colleagues suggest, the emotions of anger and resentment are not necessarily destructive; in the context of relations of care, these emotions may be productive of new forms of "long-term embodied and pragmatic responsiveness" toward others (11).

Dissociating care ethics from the strong current of idealism that has run through much of the literature over the past three decades is crucial if historical and contemporary inequalities surrounding care are to be addressed. Doing this effectively means clearly articulating care ethics as, to use Cooper's phrase (2007), "non-normative." Of course, as Cooper explains, this does not mean that normative questions are redundant. On the contrary—they are of the utmost importance. But our task is not to pronounce on ways and means of caring but to undertake an excavation of the divergent practices and norms of care that inhere in societies, including at the global level. As Cooper argues, we need to understand how they "circulate, intersect and collide" in order to understand why a particular ethos of care dominates in a particular context (258). This is particularly important when we recognize the extent to which the norms and practices of care are heavily laden with histories of oppression and subordination, as well as contemporary social relations of capitalism and patriarchy.

As care becomes transnationalized, the webs of relations that provide care and security become more complex. As care is increasingly commodified, feminized, and racialized, we must pay more attention to transnational hierarchies of gender and race, normative structures of hegemonic masculinities, and moral discourses of "womanhood," "family," "exoticism," and "national security." While practices of peace-keeping must be critically evaluated in order to avoid the dangers of "colonial care," other transnational caring practices demand similar interrogation.

A feminist ethics of care does not understand ethics as a set of principles waiting to be "applied" to a particular issue in world politics; rather, it views the task of normative or moral theory as one of *critical moral ethnography*—understanding how morality is "seated and reproduced in actual human societies" (M. Walker 1999: 211). In this view, morality is not, as Walker says, "socially modular"—on the contrary, it is embedded in the social, material, and discursive hierarchies that characterize most societies. Thus, moral standards, statuses, and distributions of responsibility must be seen as working *through* social differences rather than in spite of them (211). When "doing" ethics is understood in this way, it becomes clear that the moral theorist cannot choose to abstain from the work of *really looking* at the social, economic, and political arrangements by claiming that they are not the stuff of moral theory.

In the context of preventing conflict and building peace, reading care critically through the lens of postcolonialism means coming to terms with current patterns of domination, dependence, and interdependence by situating them within seemingly distant historical and spatial contexts. International actors must therefore recognize themselves not as external to the conflict and postconflict situations but enmeshed in them through historically and spatially expansive relations of colonialism, as well as contemporary global security governance and global political economy. This means questioning the "taken-for-granted historical geographies" that inform our analyses of security, peace, and conflict; instead, there is a need to acknowledge "the mutual constitution of Europe and the non-European world and their joint role in making history" (Barkawi and Laffey 2006: 330).

Furthermore, programs and policies undertaken in the name of care must not be styled according to Western or liberal understandings of the nature and extent of care needs but should be open to local and indigenous understandings of the requirements of and distribution of responsibility for care. For example, while liberal discourse constructs care as a temporary measure for those who cannot meet the autonomy requirements of a fully liberal society, many nonliberal understandings of care regard caring practices as empowering and as a way of critiquing prevailing discourses of race, class, and gender. Listening to and including the whole spectrum of voices on how care should be understood and how care responsibilities should be distributed are central to the building of *democratic* caring societies.

African feminisms—with their own particular understandings of ethics and care—may have particular relevance in the context of peacebuilding. Widely associated with Patricia Hill Collins, and derived from Alice Walker's term "womanist," womanism is generally used to represent the cultural, historical, and political positionality of African American woman, a group that has experienced "slavery, segregation, sexism and classism for most of its history in the United States" (Beauboeuf-Lafontant 2002: 72). Womanism may be described as a standpoint epistemology, since it ties knowledge to the experience of oppression. However, central to womanism is the understanding of oppression as a function of the convergence of racism, sexism, and classism; in other words, womanists have an "intersectional" understanding of oppression and power.

Patricia Hill Collins has argued that while white feminists have effectively confronted white male analyses of their own experience as mothers, they rarely challenge controlling images such as "the mammy, the matriarch, and the welfare mother" (1998: 118). Thus, she argues that feminist work on motherhood has failed to produce an effective critique of elite white-male and black-male analyses of black motherhood, which regularly construct black women as richly endowed with devotion, self-sacrifice, and unconditional love (118). In contrast to this, Collins demonstrates the importance of woman-centered family networks in the practice of black women's mothering, thus illustrating how traditional cultural values—namely, the African origins of community-based care—can help people cope with and resist oppression. Theoretically, this approach to care challenges the patriarchal capitalist notion of children as "private property" and is thus "revolutionary" in its challenge to notions of property, child care, and gender differences that are embedded in the institutional arrangements of any given political economy (124).

Heidi Hudson has explored the role of African feminisms in constructing a gendered approach to peacebuilding in Africa. She argues that African feminisms not only acknowledge forms of oppression other than gender; they also consider the possibility that "in that context, gender is but one unit of analysis that sometimes has to subject itself to the universal bond between men and women against racism and imperialism" (2009: 292). African feminisms also integrate into their gender analysis the traditional concept of *ubuntu*—the interconnectiveness of each human being, consensus building, and social solidarity (293). The African idea of *ubuntu* rejects the idea of a person as an independent, solitary entity. A person's humanity emerges from being "enveloped in a community of other human beings, in being caught up in the bundle of life" (Desmond Tutu, quoted in Porter 2007: 182).

Educational theorist Heidi Ross draws links between the feminist ethics of care and ideas like *ubuntu*, based on indigenous or local knowledge, as well as the more complex theories of scholars like Collins and Chandra Mohanty, who "share the project of reconceptualizing agency (and space), not as self-assertion or mastery, but as creating and sustaining relationships for change" (Ross 2002: 416). This latter group of theorists are anti-utopian in their relational analyses, arguing that relationships are enacted among individuals whose different group standpoints provide them with varying levels of power and advantage (416). Indeed, these theorists regard all relationships through the prism of historical and contemporary relations of race and colonialism; this does not mean that progressive change is impossible but rather that methods of interaction—such as "dialogue"—cannot be considered neutral or universal. Despite their diversity, all of these genres of relational thinking—care ethics, indigenous knowledges such as *ubuntu*, and black and "third-world" feminisms—use strong conceptions of relationality to illuminate "space-place" concerns and what Ross calls the "distance between us" (416).

Building on these synergies, a critical ethics of care in the context of peacebuilding is not primarily concerned with mapping out the procedures by which agreement or consensus on universalizable principles can be reached. Nor is it preoccupied with the clash between universal notions of autonomy and equality on the one hand, and justice understood as recognition of distinct identities on the other. Rather, it takes as its starting point a human ontology of relationality. It is through affective relations that all human life—including moral life—is mediated. These relations are not pristine relations of mutuality and equality. Indeed, many of them are "asymmetric relations of dependency as well as interdependencies that do not even approximate reciprocal exchanges" (M. Walker 2003: 104). In the global context, relational thinking may provide "inherent defences against Eurocentrism because it begins with the assumption that the social world is composed of relations rather than separate objects, like great powers or 'the West'" (Barkawi and Laffey 2006: 349).

Practices of care, which are central ways through which we fulfill our responsibilities to others, exist in all types of relationships. Often, responsibilities of care are ignored or evaded, leaving the vulnerable in even more desperate circumstances. In this view, building peace is about building and rebuilding relationships to ensure that adequate care is given and received. In situations of violent conflict, distributions of responsibilities and practices of care have broken down, leading to serious deficiencies in moral relations, emotional and physical well-being, and material provision. Sometimes this happens quickly, if the onset of violence is sudden; often, it happens over longer periods—years or even decades—if conflict-ridden areas have previously been plagued by poverty or other forms of structural violence. In all cases, the reconstruction of networks of relations of responsibility and care will take as long as, or longer than, the processes that led them to break down. These rebuilding processes, furthermore, will require the fostering of patience and attentiveness to the needs, fears, and hopes of others. These qualities are necessary in order to achieve trust—that moral feeling that is perhaps most fragile in postconflict situations but is crucial in ensuring that relations of care are never paternalistic, oppressive, or exploitative.

Building, and rebuilding, relations of care is a political process. It requires, at the outset, a moral and political commitment to care as the substantive basis of our moral responsibilities to others. While it has no predetermined model of how care should be delivered, it must rest on a shared commitment to prioritizing care needs and addressing the distribution of care responsibilities. This is not simply a question of justice—a question of how to divide up goods and services in a manner that is deemed "just" based on some prior principle of distribution. It is a matter of recognizing that responsibilities of care are the most basic substance of morality, as well as the most basic activity of citizenship. Peacebuilding and state building require attention to the distribution of caring responsibilities and resources among institutions on a variety of scales. To facilitate this commitment, caring practices and labor must be recognized as a vital activity of citizenship and as the most fundamental feature of well-functioning communities and states. This, in turn, requires a willingness to confront the ways deficiencies in care may be linked to historical and contemporary norms and representations of gender and race in societies, as well as to unequal and exploitation institutions and structures within political economies. It also involves a long-term process of inquiry into where and when care is deficient, as well as long-term negotiation and renegotiation of the distribution of responsibilities of care across a variety of social and political actors.

This should be read not as an attempt to reify and reinforce women's roles as nurturers or caregivers but rather as a recognition of the public and political worth of the skills gained through such roles in the context of peacebuilding. As Elisabeth Porter notes, in places such as Guatemala, Liberia, and Northern Ireland, women included in peace processes introduce issues of education, health care, employment, human rights, and land rights as integral to debates on "peace and security" primarily because of their intimate connections within families, tribes, clans, informal networks, and community groups (2007: 34). It is important to reiterate that linking the practice of building and sustaining peace to the activities of care and nurturance does not valorize these activities or the qualities required to undertake them. These claims, instead, are firmly grounded in experience—the experiences of diverse women enmeshed in a variety of webs and networks of relationships. In the wake of conflict, women and girls "continue to care for maimed loved ones, ill or old dependents and traumatized, fearful children while dealing with their own personal hurt" (38). Moreover, the emphasis on women in a caring approach to peacebuilding does not seek to single out women as suitable for these activities or to essentialize caring qualities as "feminine." The association of care with women and the feminine is constructed through cultural discourse and material social relations. It is in the critical interrogation of the discursive and material constitution of care that the transformative potential of care ethics lies.

At the Expert Group Meeting organized by UNESCO on Women's Contribution to a Culture of Peace, held in Manila, Philippines, on 25–28 April 1995, several suggestions were put forward regarding the transformation toward a culture of peace. They included consciously transforming the socialization process toward gender equity and peace through changes in the definitions of masculinity and femininity; providing open opportunities for both genders in all spheres of human endeavor; changing child-rearing practices to involve women and men equally in parenting and child care and responsibility for the welfare and education of children (Quisumbing 2000: 254). While vigilance is required to ensure that suggestions of this nature do not translate into disciplining discourses that may target certain groups of already marginalized men, they can nonetheless be important in understanding the types of transformations required to sustain peace over the long term if they focus on the institutionalization of hegemonic masculinities rather than the behaviors of individual men.

A feminist ethics of care is an important resource for conceptualizing the ethics and politics of humanitarian intervention, peacekeeping, and peacebuilding. Building on the work of feminists like Elisabeth Porter, I have sought to show how the emphasis in care ethics on the building and rebuilding of relations of responsibility and care over the long term provides a strong normative basis for the construction of a lasting, durable peace. However, there are explicit dangers in the use of care discourses, especially where the interventions of international actors are required to help keep and build peace. Care discourses can quickly translate into paternalistic discourses of benevolence in which the powerful care for inferior others who lack the ability to act as autonomous agents. This discourse of paternalistic caring is particularly dangerous in the context of peacebuilding, where societies and their members are usually dislocated, hurt, and vulnerable.

I have suggested, however, that there are alternatives to the paternalistic ethics of care. In the context of peacebuilding, a fully feminist ethics of care that is attuned to historical and contemporary relations of interdependence disrupts and challenges conventional understandings of domination and dependence. Here, international peacebuilding efforts are contextualized through relations of colonialism and neocolonialism. These actors cannot, then, isolate themselves from local conflicts but must understand conflicts as historically linked to previous patterns of interdependence. While this will certainly involve the full inclusion of women in peacebuilding activities, it will not essentialize women's roles as caregivers. Rather, a critical ethics of care reveals the importance of adequate provision for care for lasting peace but at the same time interrogates existing distributions of care and care work.

6 | Health and Human Security

Gender, Care, and HIV/AIDS

This chapter considers HIV/AIDS in the context of human security by using the lens of the feminist ethics of care. The ethics of care refers to a moral framework characterized by an ontological commitment to relationality and care as the basis of human well-being. This leads to the weak normative position that enhancing and supporting equitable and adequate relations of care at all levels of human interaction are key to mitigating insecurity in many sectors of life. An examination of the global HIV/AIDS pandemic using this lens—with a focus on sub-Saharan Africa—reveals largely hidden aspects of human insecurity in this context: the fundamental need of those suffering from AIDS-related disease for constant, day-to-day care in order to ensure not only their security but their survival; the economic and physical insecurity experienced by caregivers—largely women—in HIV/AIDS–affected households; and the caring burden placed on vulnerable groups, especially elderly women, seeking to manage the orphan crisis. Although many organizations and much research concerning AIDS now explicitly recognize the role played by women in home-based caregiving, and the effects of this caregiving on their economic and physical security, gender and care work remains an "issue" related to HIV/AIDS and women rather than used as a framework through which to view the relationship between gender, HIV/AIDS, and human security.

While it is widely recognized that poverty exacerbates the effects of HIV/AIDS on households and communities, this fact is seldom explored in relation to the hidden "care economy" and the gendered global political economy more broadly. Similarly, while there is increasing recognition of the link between violence against women and women's vulnerability to HIV/AIDS, a feminist ethics of care reveals the links between these trends and the widespread degradation of the values and practices of caring, and the valorization of forms of hegemonic masculinity. The structures and institutions of militarism, the continuum of violence against women, and threats to women's sexual and reproductive health matter profoundly for human security—*not just for women* but for all people. In this context, reducing levels of both conventional and structural violence globally depends, in part, upon a transformation of the norms that denigrate and feminize the values and labor of care while underwriting the gendered processes of globalization and militarism.

I begin with a critical analysis of HIV/AIDS as a "security issue." I argue that conceptualizing the global AIDS crisis through security lenses has so far failed to highlight many crucial aspects of how this crisis actually plays out in the context of people's real lives and how it may affect their security. This is true of both the "securitization" of AIDS, which frames the crisis in national security terms, and much of the human security literature, especially that which focuses on good governance and individual human rights. While some of the critical human security approaches do recognize the fundamental contradiction between basic human well-being and many central aspects of contemporary global restructuring, most fail to consider the key role played by gender relations and the global care economy in determining the nature and distribution of the effects of this neoliberal restructuring.

I then explore the relationship between gender relations and the HIV/AIDS pandemic by using the lens of a critical feminist ethics of care. First, I examine the impact of HIV/AIDS on caregiving in situations of extreme poverty by offering a detailed account of the nature, distribution, and effects of AIDS care, focusing on the situation in sub-Saharan Africa. I argue that the implications of the care burden go beyond merely "increased labor" and include income loss, serious physical and psychosocial health risks for carers, breakdown of household relations, and erosion of the social fabric of communities. The fact that women and girls are the primary home caregivers for AIDS sufferers around the world must be linked to wider questions surrounding the global care economy and global economic restructuring.

I first concentrate primarily on the material conditions and impact of the HIV/AIDS care crisis and then blend material and discursive analysis to provide an analysis of the link between hegemonic masculinities and forms of HIV/AIDS–related violence. Specifically, I examine violence against women, which includes violence in the home and militarized sexual violence, in relation to HIV/AIDS. Addressing gender-based violence in terms of hegemonic masculinities and the feminization of care can shed light on the significance of gender relations in transforming cultures of violence and enhancing security for women, men, and children who are living with the realities of HIV/AIDS.

HIV/AIDS and Security

Since 2000, there has been a growing trend toward the framing of HIV/AIDS as a security issue, starting with the official designation by the UN Security Council of HIV/AIDS as a threat to international peace and security in Africa (Elbe 2006: 121). Clearly, there are ethical and policy dangers involved in the framing of HIV/AIDS as a "national security" issue in realist terms. As Tony Barnett argues, the use of security language suggests that the effects of the epidemic are important only insofar as they supposedly pose a threat to a particular state or group of states (2006: 297). This then creates a danger that international efforts to stem the pandemic may become motivated by narrow national interests rather than "altruism" (Elbe 2006: 120). For example, Stefan Elbe argues that what he calls "securitization" could "push national and international responses to the disease away from civil society towards state institutions," including the military, with the power to override the human rights and civil liberties of those living with HIV/AIDS; he suggests that, tied to this, securitization may prioritize AIDS funding to armed forces and elites and that the discourse of "threat" may work against the efforts of those seeking to "normalize social perceptions" regarding persons living with HIV/AIDS (120).

Despite these arguments, the possible instrumental benefits of linking HIV/AIDS to national security have not gone unnoticed. Indeed, especially in the heightened, post-9/11 security climate, this move could potentially raise awareness of the pandemic and bolster resources for international AIDS initiatives (Elbe 2006: 120). However, given the possibility for misunderstanding of the nature and effects of the virus and its related illnesses, misplaced values regarding the best methods for combating medical, social, political, and economic problems associated with the disease, and the possible misdirection of resources, many critics are left wondering whether or not the "securitization" path may do more harm than good.

Interestingly, in his 2006 article, Elbe uses the term "securitization" simply to refer to the process whereby an issue comes to be recognized in "security" terms. He does not, however, explicitly address the critical literature on "securitization," which focuses on the discursive logic and political (or "depoliticizing") implications of this move. As discussed previously, for critical security theorists—especially of the Copenhagen school—the framing of an issue in security terms represents not simply a policy decision; rather, it is a discursive move, or "speech act," which essentially removes that issue from the realm of normal, day-to-day politics, casting it as an "existential threat" calling for and justifying extreme measures (M. Williams 1998: 435). Other critical theorists have focused less on the discursive acts and more on the security practices of security agencies; in this view, policing insecurity is thus a mode of governmentality that seeks to monopolize the truth about danger (c.a.s.e. collective 2006: 457). While Elbe does not elaborate on the term "securitization" with respect to HIV/AIDS, his 2005 article "AIDS, Security, Biopolitics" does address the biopolitical dimensions of the securitization of AIDS—specifically, the licensing of the detailed monitoring and surveillance of the world population, the governing of "life"—in relation to HIV/AIDS (404–405). These security practices are connected to the multiple forms of security associated with AIDS: national, international, and human.

Ever since the concept of "human security" began to take shape, there has been widespread recognition that HIV/AIDS and its associated social, political, and economic effects constituted a serious human security crisis. Certainly, it could be argued that this recognition has been set back by the recent challenge to the initial, broad United Nations Development Program (UNDP) formulation of human security as "freedom from want" by the narrower "freedom from fear" formulation; even so, there remains a strong sense, among many theorists and advocates, that HIV/AIDS should be understood as a human security issue because of its direct threat to human life and because of the other threats that the disease poses to human safety and well-being (see Tiessen 2006). However, there may be problems with this formulation; as Colleen O'Manique argues, enveloping HIV/AIDS within a human security framework may mask the extent to which prevailing policies and practices of global governance may sustain and even deepen the security crisis of HIV/AIDS in sub-Saharan Africa (2006: 162). I next address the HIV/AIDS epidemic in the context of human security in order to understand what it means to think about HIV/AIDS as a human security crisis, in both moral and practical terms.

Health, HIV/AIDS, and Human Security

Since the emergence of the human security paradigm, global health has increasingly been drawn into the discourse (Chen and Narasimhan 2003: 186). As Chen and Narasimhan point out, at the simplest level, premature and unnecessary loss of life is perhaps the greatest insecurity of human life (183). However, it is increasingly recognized that the relationship between health and human security is more complex than this. The human security paradigm recognizes the connections between poverty, health, and insecurity. Moreover, violent conflict and complex humanitarian situations reveal the complexity of the relationship between health and security; as Chen and Narasimhan explain, conflicts often expose the long neglect of basic public health services in which the social trust that underlies health services has eroded (186).

Beyond poverty and violence, global infectious disease has also powerfully influenced thinking about the linkage between human security and global health. Indeed, it has been argued that the global HIV/AIDS pandemic has been a major driver linking health to human security (Chen and Narasimhan 2003). The human security paradigm provides a framework for considering HIV/AIDS within the context of security while avoiding many of the potential dangers of "securitization" associated with the realist, national security paradigm. Because the human security approach widely advocates shifting the primary referent of security away from states and toward individuals, the security implications of HIV/AIDS are no longer about national militaries and state survival, or about AIDS-devastated communities being "breeding grounds" for terrorism; on the contrary, the focus shifts toward *human* insecurity and vulnerability to AIDS and its effects on communities (O'Manique 2006: 161, emphasis added). But the human security implications of HIV/AIDS go beyond "health," narrowly understood; the HIV/AIDS pandemic, especially in the world's poorest regions, has had devastating effects on economic security, food security, and peacemaking and peacebuilding capacity in conflict and postconflict zones (see Tiessen 2006).

Colleen O'Manique takes up this challenge in the context of HIV/AIDS and human security. She argues that while human security advocates often champion liberal values and the need to spread democracy and good governance, there is little questioning of the extent to which a particular set of neoliberal values, policies and practices "nourish and sustain the security crisis of HIV/AIDS . . . and shape institutional responses to the pandemic" (2006: 162). While she is concerned with the continual violation of basic rights precipitated by the AIDS crisis, she locates those rights within a "broader systemic and global crisis of social reproduction." Seen in this way, it is not surprising that, as O'Manique points out, the effects of this epidemic are felt most profoundly by women, who face specific difficulties protecting themselves from infection and who must shoulder the burden of daily household reproduction, including the care of the sick (162). Indeed, she argues that "women's 'private' and care giving labour, the very basis of human security," is taken for granted, rendered invisible, viewed as "natural" (169). Furthermore, she points out that women's experiences of violence in sub-Saharan Africa are not understood in relation to broader social and cultural norms governing gender relations (169). The ethical lens of care ethics brings women's "invisible" labor into view and highlights the implications for economic and health security for those who are infected and ill, those who care for them, and the entire network of family and community that is affected. Furthermore, as a feminist perspective, it reveals the feminization of care work as anything but natural and questions the privatization and devaluation of this most fundamental human activity. Finally, it may help to reveal why the distancing of men from caring activities is related to constructions of masculinity and femininity, which may contribute to the proliferation of violence both within and outside the household.

To develop these important insights regarding gender and global restructuring on the human security implications of HIV/AIDS, I focus in particular on the material aspects of women's caregiving labor and the discursive implications of hegemonic masculinities and violence. I use the ontological and ethical lens of care in order to more clearly elucidate how different forms of institutional, structural, and discursive power are exercised through various patterns and distributions of responsibility. These patterns and distributions of responsibility determine whose security is compromised by HIV/AIDS and how, precisely, their security is affected. I argue that an ethics of care perspective can illuminate the structural, material, and "cultural" determinants that affect how families and households living with HIV/AIDS negotiate their moral responsibilities, as well as offer a new perspective on the moral crises and demands created by the HIV/AIDS pandemic in the poorest parts of the world.

Care Work in HIV/AIDS Households

We stand together in the shared values of grassroots women caring for their families and communities, but against these roles and contributions being detrimental to the health and well-being of these women, their families and communities.

—STATEMENT OF THE GRASSROOTS ACADEMY, YWCA INTERNATIONAL WOMEN'S SUMMIT, NAIROBI, KENYA, JULY 2007

The 2008 UNAIDS *Report on the Global AIDS Epidemic* states that women account for two-thirds of all caregivers for people living with HIV in Africa. This statistic is supported by a survey conducted for the Henry J. Kaiser Family Foundation, which surveyed 771 AIDS-affected households in South Africa. The study found that 68 percent of the caregivers in the households surveyed were women or girls—7 percent of them younger than eighteen years and 23 percent older than sixty years. Furthermore, it found that more than 40 percent of households reported that the primary caregiver had taken time off from formal or informal employment or schooling to take care of the person sick with AIDS, adding to the loss of household income and the underschooling of girls (Steinberg et al. 2002: ii).

Care work in this context includes a wide variety of activities, including physical, clinical, psychosocial, emotional, spiritual, financial, and practical care (Mehta and Gupta 2006: 15). Of course, many individuals infected with HIV, as well as those suffering from AIDS-related illness, receive care from formal, usually national, health-care services. However, it is widely recognized that the cumulative effects of increasing HIV sero-prevalence in highly affected countries has resulted in unprecedented demands being placed on already under-resourced health-care services. Moreover, in many countries, these services have been further weakened by health-sector reform and structural adjustment programs (Ogden, Esim, and Grown 2006: 336). In addition, it must be recognized that the number of people obtaining an HIV diagnosis are a minority of the total number infected (UNAIDS 2008). Many of those who suspect that they have HIV may lack access to or avoid public health care because of stigma, ignorance, or fear. Thus, as Ogden, Esim, and Grown conclude, the majority of those affected are being cared for by family members—mostly women—at home (336).

In most countries of high HIV prevalence, women are already performing much of the daily, non-HIV/AIDS-related care work. When HIV/AIDS enters the home, women's care work burden increases exponentially, which can compromise their health and their ability to generate income and participate in education, skill building, and other markers of well-being (UNAIDS 2008: 168). Moreover, most women in these countries are performing these tasks under conditions of moderate to severe poverty. There is little moral or material support for their work, in the form of training, medication and medical supplies, support from formal programs, and school support for children. Finally, they themselves may also be sick with AIDS-related illnesses, or they may become sick with other illnesses as they are forced to neglect their own health (Mehta and Gupta 2006: 6–7).

Mehta and Gupta summarize just some of the mammoth tasks carried out by home caregivers where members are suffering from AIDS-related illness:

> For a bed-ridden family member, this may involve bathing, toilet assistance, turning (to avoid bedsores), providing water and nutrition. It may additionally require accompanying the patient to the hospital, bringing food to the hospital and supplementing nursing care. Furthermore, patients are often depressed and stigmatized, requiring the carer to provide counseling and moral support. Marital conflict and relationships may be strained as households grapple with the effects of poverty exacerbated by the disease. (16)

Among the most striking findings of the Kaiser Family Foundation survey report is that the households worst affected by HIV/AIDS are those most underserved by basic public services such as sanitation and piped water. They found that only 43 percent of households in the survey had a tap in the dwelling, and nearly a quarter of the rural households in the survey had no toilet at all (Steinberg et al. 2002: ii). Consider, in addition, the following findings: "Roughly one in six individuals could not control their bowels (16%) and fractionally more lacked bladder control. About 17% needed help to get on or off the toilet, and getting in and out of bed. Approximately one in five people could not wash without assistance (19%) while just over 17% had to be helped to dress. One person in ten had to be helped to eat" (13). As the authors of the study point out, under even the best of circumstances, lack of control over bodily functions is humiliating for the patient and unpleasant for the carer. But "when access to a toilet is difficult and there are not proper facilities for the safe disposal of fecal matter, conditions are so much more miserable, and there is high risk for contamination and infection of others as well" (13).

Very little is known about the ways in which providing care for an HIV-positive patient affects the working lives of caregivers and their ability to financially support and care for their healthy family members (Rajaraman, Earle, and Heymann 2008: 3). What little research exists demonstrates that the effects are not trivial; indeed, a number of small studies in East Africa have suggested that household food security and material well-being may be negatively affected by disruptions in work and domestic responsibilities among HIV caregivers (3).

In a study of AIDS-affected households in Kagabiro village in Tanzania, an average of 29 percent of household labor was devoted to AIDS-related care. In two-thirds of the cases included in the study, each household had two women devoted to AIDS care, and the total labor lost to households was 43 percent (Tibaijuka 1997: 968). This study also demonstrates how the reallocation of labor by women from economic activities to caring for the sick has had negative effects on food security. Sixty percent of the households in the study considered food security in jeopardy because young women no longer produce as many supplementary root crops as they did before (972). Indeed, the authors of a 2003 article in the *Lancet* present evidence that the new aspects to the food crisis in Africa that can be attributed largely to the HIV/AIDS epidemic in the region constitute what they call "new variant famine." They argue that the general burden of care in both AIDS-affected and non-AIDS-affected households has reduced the viability of farming livelihoods and increased the prospects for a sharp decline into severe famine (De Waal and Whiteside 2003).

Moreover, the low-income base of the society in this study, combined with the high material costs in terms of reduced production due to loss of labor, means that impoverishment occurs not only at household but also at community levels, thereby reducing the chances for the bereaved to obtain community support (Tibaijuka 1997: 972). AIDS has contributed greatly to the crippling of the system of support by extended families and communities that have historically been a survival net in many parts of Africa. Ogden, Esim, and Grown cite a study by Seeley et al. (1993: 122) that found that "blanket statements about the role of the extended family in Africa as a safety net need to be questioned and assumptions that the extended family will be ready and able to assist sick members, treated with caution" (Ogden, Esim, and Grown 2006: 336).

As this study points out, while Western gender stereotypes may paint a picture of women HIV caregivers as "stay-at-home" carers whose spouses are employed outside the home, the reality is far different. Indeed, a very large number of AIDS caregivers are also working outside the home. Women constitute a substantial part of the global workforce beyond the care economy—in both the informal and formal sectors of paid labor. They are already clustered in the lowest-paid, most insecure sectors—the service sector; the highly competitive urban informal sector; agriculture, where marketing of cash crops is often dominated by men; and the formal sector in the lower-paying jobs (UNFPA 2006c).

The Ethics of Care, HIV/AIDS, and Human Security

Clearly, the material burden of HIV/AIDS, particularly on women, is vast. But how does this burden relate to security, and human security in particular? How should all of this be considered from an ethical perspective? What kinds of moral questions should we ask, and what sorts of moral issues are raised when we consider women's care work in the context of HIV/AIDS? If the HIV/AIDS crisis is a crisis of human security, how can we make sense of the moral challenges to which we must respond?

Commonly, when thinking ethically about any kind of mass suffering—global poverty, for example—we tend to ask questions about who is responsible for this suffering and, occasionally (although less frequently), what can be done to alleviate it. The latter is asked less often because it invariably involves thinking about practical measures to address the situation "on the ground," all of which is seen to be outside the scope of moral reasoning. In addition, when we consider what it is we are trying to alleviate or restore, we generally frame the discussion by using the discourse of individual human rights. Rights are seen as being violated in such contexts, and rights are what must be restored.

But the illustrations given previously regarding the everyday struggles of families and communities dealing with HIV/AIDS demonstrates a different side to morality. Here it is possible to see with great clarity the extent to which responsibilities arise out of attachments and connections with particular others. For those who have family members or other close friends living with the disease, acting morally involves cultivating virtues of patience and attentiveness. While it may mean making moral decisions about where to concentrate one's energies and resources—especially when there are children living in an HIV-infected household—care ethics suggests that, often, morality is more about a complex long-term narrative of balancing needs and priorities rather than a series of isolated moral choices. In this sense, acting "morally" involves sustained responsiveness to particular others with whom one exists in close personal—usually familial—relations. Furthermore, for those suffering from AIDS-related illness, relations of trust must be fostered with caregivers, on whom they are largely dependent during this period of their lives.

In this sense, while I agree with Virginia Held that the ethics of care must focus on the "compelling moral salience of attending to and meeting the needs of particular others for whom we take responsibility" (2006: 10), I argue that this alone is an inadequate vision for the ethics of care. To think usefully about ethics, and care ethics in particular, we must remember that the nature of relations of care and practices of responsibility are constructed and performed according to certain norms and structures that change over space and time. Thus, when we think about who is caring for whom today, we realize that it is no longer simply a question of mothers caring for their own children within the localized space of the home. Indeed, it is no longer immediately obvious what we mean when we say "others for whom we take responsibility." Care now is transnational. Care work is a fundamental component of the global political economy. Therefore, an ethics of care cannot afford to be a private or personal ethics. On the contrary, it must be a global, political ethics.

These developments can be seen clearly in the context of HIV/AIDS. Here, the moral responsibilities of care stretch beyond personal and familial ties. HIV/AIDS affects households, but it also affects, and is affected by, relations within extended families, communities, nation-states, and the global political economy. While households must make moral decisions about the organization of care, so, too, must communities and nation-states. Moreover, these decisions are always made within the constraints and context of global economic governance, geopolitics, and "cultural" norms about gender, race, and the role and nature of caring. From the perspective of a critical feminist ethics of care, these moral decisions cannot and should not be made without careful consideration of the specific social and personal relations and how each will be affected. Determining the nature, amount, and distribution of care at these different levels is not merely a question of distributive justice.

Orphaned children of varying ages, for example, may benefit from a variety of different care arrangements; determining what is appropriate in these cases will involve consideration, and sometimes critical interrogation, of a wide variety of social norms and values. Moreover, from the perspective of care, ensuring human security in the context of HIV/AIDS devastation requires consideration of those experiencing the set of needs embodied in care and the actors who seek or are assigned to satisfy those needs (Daly 2002: 268). Grandmothers who take on the role of primary carer of infants and young children are themselves in need of specific kinds of care—care that may often be overlooked where there are others who are deemed "more vulnerable."

Thus, considering human security through the lens of care ethics would refocus our attention on the intersecting contexts and conditions that lead to a variety of harms rather than on the achievement of a series of overarching political objectives. Instead of concentrating primarily, for example, on the formal institutions of democracy and the universal legal rights of all individuals—to privacy, to land, to access to medications—this approach focuses more on the particular contexts in which people are experiencing insecurity in the context of HIV/AIDS. Who—which humans—are experiencing insecurity? How do different factors relating to who those people are—women or men, young or old, patient or carer (or both)—affect the nature of their insecurity? How does their illness, or their extra caring labor, affect their ability to work in paid labor and thus provide for their families? How does the wider socioeconomic context—at the national and global levels—work either with or against policies or projects of this nature designed to increase levels of security? How do existing cultural norms and discursive constructions of gender, race, and ethnicity, as well as the existing political culture on the legitimacy of care, affect the balance of the role of the state and private institutions—including the household—in providing that care?

The cycle of chronic illness and death that is the HIV/AIDS crisis is destroying already fragile networks of support, mutual responsiveness, and caring. This destruction, when coupled with neoliberal austerity measures; patriarchal social structures, including militarism; and local and global norms of hegemonic masculinity, perpetuate other cycles of gender oppression, violence, and poverty. Clearly, men and women experience insecurity in this context in different ways; women, including very elderly and very young women, bear an enormous proportion of the care burden. This affects their health, economic and food security, rights to land and home, and ability to pursue education. Women are also more vulnerable to male violence, especially in highly militarized societies. This, too, may be understood through the lens of care; the feminization and degradation of caring values and activities do not simply run parallel to patriarchy, hegemonic masculinity, and male violence. On the contrary, the feminization of care may license, legitimize, and foster a culture of violence among men, and masculinized institutions, that is defined by the absence of relational values of empathy, mutual responsiveness, and attentiveness to the needs of others.

Confronting Hegemonic Masculinities: Violence, Militarism, and HIV/AIDS

Because there is an increasing tendency to view HIV/AIDS as a global security issue, it is not surprising that the effects of HIV on national militaries are gaining attention. The 2008 UNAIDS report on the global AIDS epidemic indicates that many national militaries, especially in the most heavily affected countries, are struggling to manage the administrative, practical, and operational issues associated with high levels of HIV infection among military personnel (176).

UNAIDS reports substantial resources being directed toward HIV prevention and treatment services throughout military structures in a number of countries. These resources are coming from state budgets and international donors, including the U.S. Department of Defense HIV/AIDS Prevention Program. In Kenya, for example, the national armed forces provided antiretroviral drugs in 2007 to an estimated 90 percent of military personnel in need and has provided voluntary counseling and testing to thousands of civilians who live near the military's seventeen designated testing sites (176).

The true realities of sexual and gender-based violence during all stages of conflict are just now becoming known. In many recent conflicts, women's bodies have become battlegrounds, as sexual violence is used as a weapon of war. Sexual violence is also common during postconflict periods and particularly in refugee situations. Less well known, however, is that rates of violence between intimate partners increase dramatically in countries devastated by war (UNFPA 2006b). This "everyday" violence against women contributes dramatically to women's vulnerability to HIV. In fact, in several African countries, the risk of HIV among women who have experienced gender-based violence may be as much as three times higher than among those who have not (Global Coalition on Women and AIDS 2006).

UNAIDS (2008) advocates a combination of social/normative learning and legal reforms as strategies for reducing gender-based violence. Similarly, a recent publication by the United Nations Population Fund suggests that both women and men must nurture and support positive expressions of masculinity and promote the core concepts of inner strength, respect, and care for partners and children. Specifically, they argue that expanding the role of boys and men within families can be achieved by fostering men's understanding of responsibility and by engaging them more fully in child care and care for the sick. This contributes to families and communities being able to deal more equitably as well as more effectively with the burdens of the epidemic (UNFPA 2006a).

While these kinds of arguments do point to the need for cultural shifts in dominant norms of gender relations at both the household and the wider societal levels, too much emphasis on "men's violence" in the context of HIV/AIDS and on "expanding the role of boys and men within families" can also be dangerous. Bringing the language of care into debates on social reproduction and security must not simply be an excuse to reprivatize care and to justify it through an increased role for men within that sphere. While this may be part of the solution, attention must be paid to the role of neighborhood, community, and state institutions, as well as to private organizations at a variety of levels, in distributing the responsibilities for care. Moreover, while the attempt to foster new relations of care among men and their families may do something to alleviate the burden of care for women, it does not address the normative and structural conditions that give rise to the feminization of care.

Toward a Caring Approach to Global Health Security

The devastating human consequences of HIV/AIDS in sub-Saharan Africa bring to light most vividly the perils of "individualistic" approaches to human security. Conceptual frameworks that posit the individual as the primary referent of human security, or rights-based ethical frameworks that valorize autonomy and concentrate on the delivery of individual human rights, fail to see the importance of relationality and the moral value of responsibilities of care toward particular others. Care in the context of AIDS is not a trivial or even secondary matter. It is a matter of life and death, and its crisis in this context constitutes an existential threat not only to the most vulnerable populations but also to entire societies, especially but not exclusively, in southern Africa.

The relational context of care provides an ontological basis from which to conceptualize the ethics of HIV/AIDS, and human security more broadly. This is not to say that human rights issues related to HIV/AIDS—concerning stigma, access to antiretrovirals, and basic health care—are unimportant. Similarly, women's legal rights—especially to property and inheritance, to education, and to equity of access for women in HIV treatment and care—are crucial in the context of AIDS (Strickland 2004). However, these rights are most usefully understood as "relational" and must be located within the wider context of care. For example, the problem of stigma must not be regarded simply as a problem for individuals infected with HIV or suffering from AIDS-related illnesses; it must also be recognized that one of the most disabling effects of stigma is that it can prevent so-called unlinked carers from reaching out for support even when it is available in their communities (Ogden, Esim, and Grown 2006: 335). Similarly, a care perspective does not preclude attention to, for example, how women's inability to exercise their property and inheritance rights affects their vulnerability to HIV. However, as reports on this issue indicate, the main effect of the violation of these rights concerns the extent to which women—who are usually the primary caregivers in AIDS-affected households, and may in fact be the only adult in the household—are better able to mitigate the negative social and economic consequences of HIV/AIDS (Strickland 2004: 10). Thus, legal reform may be seen as a crucial tool in a wider ontological commitment to recognizing our relational existence, and a normative strategy that prioritizes well-resourced networks and equitable relationships of adequate care.

I have used the case of HIV/AIDS in sub-Saharan Africa to demonstrate the transformative potential of reconceptualizing the normative basis of human security based on the ethics of care. To do so, I have drawn on widely recognized aspects of care ethics, including the relational ontology and the critique of liberal notions of autonomy, and the recognition of the "compelling moral salience of attending to and meeting the needs of the particular others for whom we take responsibility" (Held 2006: 10). Also integral to my approach, however, is the recognition that moral relations of care are constructed by the norms and structures of gender, race, global geopolitics, and capitalism. Such an approach refuses to regard ethics as "socially modular" (see M. Walker 1998) and is concerned with the interrogation of how power functions *through* ethics and how power relations—both material and ideational—provide the context in which ethical arrangements are embedded.

Addressing human security effectively in the context of the AIDS pandemic in southern Africa demands sustained, critical attention to the politics of gender relations. Understanding hegemonic forms of masculinity helps to explain the widespread existence of patriarchal households and the feminization of care work. These norms of masculinity help us understand the reasons for the concentration of women in care work; however, they can also help explain the culture that underwrites widespread male disassociation with the activities and emotions associated with care. This disconnect can take the form of neglect or violence. This violence is manifest on an individual level in the sexual and other gender-related violence of men against women and other "feminized" others; it is manifest at the institutional level in the form of militarized violence, both the "legitimate" violence of state militaries and militarized solutions to political crises, and the "illegitimate" violence of soldiers against women in conflict and postconflict situations.

Furthermore, when applied critically to the issue of human security, the ethics of care and the practices of caring should be understood in the wider contexts of the global care economy within wider trends of neoliberal global restructuring as they operate in both local and global contexts. Feminist economists, global political economists, and sociologists have convincingly shown how and why unpaid or underpaid care work—performed largely by women—demands a rethinking of traditional theories of economics, global political economy, and globalization. The importance of this labor for human security is slowly being recognized, but as Truong et al. argue, the battle is uphill: "The human security approach has yet to free itself from the regnant tendency in neoliberal reforms which tends to apply primarily male norms in valuing and regulating social life, obliterating the significance of arrangements which provide care for the very young, sick and elderly" (2006: xx).

Perhaps nowhere is this critique brought to life more vividly than in the context of HIV/AIDS in southern Africa. The overwhelming and unequal burden of care constitutes a deep and ongoing threat to the human security of many groups of people: of these women and other male carers; of those suffering from AIDS-related illnesses for whom they care; and of the vulnerable children and orphans of those who are chronically ill or deceased. On a macrolevel, it constitutes a human security threat to entire communities for which the fabric of social relations has been violently torn apart. It is woven into the gender norms governing sexual relations within households and in militarized conflict situations, as well as into the material and institutional structure of the contemporary global political economy.

While this chapter concentrates on care and security in relation to HIV/AIDS, the feminist lens of care ethics can illuminate the nature of threats to human security in a wide variety of health contexts. Maternal health, while showing some modest signs of improvement, continues to be an enormous challenge in poor countries. A 2008 study estimates 342,900 maternal deaths in that year. Of course, HIV is an important factor here; without HIV, the number of maternal deaths in 2008 would have been 281,500 (Horton 2010: 1581). A feminist ethics of care would focus attention on the relational nature of maternal health in the context of human security. A 2006 article in the *Lancet* reports that good maternal health is crucial for the welfare of the whole household, especially children who are dependent on their mothers to provide food, care, and emotional support. The death or chronic ill health of a mother increases the probability of death and poor growth and development of her children (Filippi et al. 2006: 1535–1536). Moreover, it is important to be aware of the relationships between maternal health and other aspects of women's sexual and reproductive well-being, including the prevalence of rape and sexual violence. As long as sexual violence against women continues, access to safe abortions will be a key component of health security for women around the world.

Strategies for change in the area of health must include the prioritization of questions regarding arrangements for care—the distribution of care work, the provision of care services, the removal of prohibitive financial barriers to care, such as user fees, especially in developing countries. Consideration must be given to the links between legal, political, and economic arrangements on the one hand, and the adequacy of care, especially for vulnerable groups, on the other. In pursuing these strategies, however, we must remember that women caregivers are not helpless victims; they are agents who are not only overcoming overwhelming duress to sustain families and communities on a day-to-day basis but also organizing at the grassroots level to assist and strengthen their community-based capacity for care and overall security.

7 | Gender, Care, and the Ethics of Environmental Security

From the earliest attempts at rethinking the concept of "security"—in both the academic community and at the United Nations—"the environment" has occupied a central position in these revised and expanded understandings. The defining UNDP *Human Development Report* of 1994 articulated seven dimensions of human security, one of which was environmental security. Since that time, academics have begun interrogating the security dimensions of environmental change; much of this literature has either integrated the environment into a broad concept of human security or placed environmental security as a pillar alongside human, societal, and gender security (J. Barnett 2001; Oswald Spring 2009; Dalby 2002, 2009).

In this chapter, I argue that environmental security should not be seen as distinct from other aspects of human security but as an integral part of it. Recognition of the mutual constitution of the human and natural worlds is a prerequisite to the development of an approach to human security based on the ethics and politics of care. While I am mindful of the fact that green theorists have usefully pointed out the dangers of anthropocentrism, I do not put forward an ethics of "caring for the environment." Care ethics understands morality as located in responsibilities and practices of care among human beings in the context of webs and networks of relationships. From this perspective, moral relations of care cannot be established with inanimate things or features of the natural environment, such as rocks, trees, or lakes.[1] Rather, seen through the lens of care ethics, the health and flourishing of the natural environment must be understood as inextricably connected with the health and flourishing of persons. Our ability to care for each other depends fundamentally upon our ability to maintain a healthy natural environment.

This is not an instrumental view of nature; rather, it simply suggests that we can make moral sense of the environment only in the context of our association with it. Thus, while humans do not have morally based relations of care with the natural environment, the care that is taken to protect the environment, in conjunction with our caring for other persons, relies on an awareness that adequate and nonoppressive care may require acting with restraint and patience. An ethics of care recognizes the fundamental importance of a healthy biosphere not insofar as it can service our appetites for consumption but insofar as we must work with, in, and through the natural environment in order to give and receive care adequately, and in order to create and maintain a secure and sustainable home for ourselves and future generations.

Environmental Security

Like human security, the idea of environmental security is relatively new. Indeed, it is a concept that has entered the lexicons of security studies and environmental studies only since the late 1980s—thus emerging just slightly earlier than, and developing almost concurrently

---

[1] Certainly there are instances of relations of mutual care among human beings and animals. Many house pets, especially dogs, provide comfort and even care for their owners that is reciprocated and crucial to the flourishing and the emotional health of both pet and owner. More specifically, service dogs—for people who are blind or for autistic children—perform functions of care for specific persons and likely receive care from the individuals and families with whom they live. However, this, too, remains outside the analytical and ethical framework of a critical ethics of care, because it is neither shaped by discursive and ideational norms regarding gender, race, and the role of care in society nor by the material limitations of the global economy. This is not to say, however, that there are no political questions surrounding service dogs, including who is responsible for providing and resourcing, and which individuals qualify to receive, this service.

with, human security (J. Barnett 2007: 4). Not surprisingly, however, there is no agreed-upon definition of environmental security or of environmental insecurity (Dalby 2002). As is the case with other "new" security fields—such as health—it has been suggested that the "securitization" of the environment is largely a rhetorical device used to "imbue a sense of urgency and priority to nature." The idea is that by naming something as a security threat, it will be able to command greater political priority and larger resource allocations (Khagram, Clark, and Raad 2003: 292). Daniel Deudney also points out that the term "environmental security" has been used to "mobilize and motivate," redirecting social energies toward environmental amelioration" (2006: 245).

While this discursive strategy may appear to be nothing but beneficial for the goals of environmental sustainability and conservation, advocates are wary of the potential dangers of linking the environment to security. Again, paralleling the case of health security described earlier, there is some fear that deploying the rhetoric of environmental security will serve only to "militarize the environment," making environmental politics "more conflictual and parochial" (Deudney 2006: 245). Of course, this is especially the case when environmental scarcity and degradation are linked to state or "national" security, and security is understood primarily in terms of risks and threats linked to violent conflict and militarized responses. The strongest of these arguments suggests that there is a causal relationship between environmental degradation, resource scarcity, and violent conflict; this claim supports the argument that there is a potential role for the military and other security institutions with respect to environmental protection. The link between the environment and conventional notions of national security was first put forward at the end of the Cold War, a time when scholars and policy analysts were searching for new threats and security priorities around which to build security policy. This wave of thinking is often said to have culminated in Robert Kaplan's essay "The Coming Anarchy," which described "the environment" as "the national-security issue of the early twenty-first century" (1994: 58).

This view remains remarkably widespread in policy discourse and the public imagination, despite evidence to the contrary. As Simon Dalby points out, "The scholarly literature that suggests that environmental changes rarely cause conflict directly and only occasionally do so indirectly (Kahl 2006) doesn't get as much attention in the media as the more alarmist claims about imminent crisis" (2009: 3). Thomas Homer-Dixon's work, however, demonstrates effectively that although resource scarcity can contribute to "civil violence, including insurgencies and ethnic clashes, many of the sweeping claims about immanent inter-state resource wars, or environmental wars between the North and the South, were unfounded" (1999: 177). Indeed, recent research on the effects of violent conflict on the environment have "reversed the causal arrows of analysis, as cases of the negative impacts of military activities and warfare on the environment are abundant" (Khagram, Clark, and Raad 2003: 293). This suggests, maybe paradoxically, that military activities—perhaps carried out in the name of security—may be one of the greatest threats to environmental security, understood in terms of human security.

Environmental security has been one of the key categories of human security since the UNDP 1994 *Human Development Report*. As Dalby argues, although this document offered neither obvious priorities for policy nor an effective lens through which research could be conducted, the 1994 report made a clear link between human security and the environment, and this link would prove to subsequently influence many researchers (2009: 43). Jon Barnett, for example, emphasizes the normative nature of a human-centered environmental security concept. This understanding sees the enhancement of welfare, peace, and justice as the fundamental purpose of politics (2001: 127). While his conceptualization of human security is "very much about the rights of all people to a healthy environment," he argues that rights are "meaningless" without responsibilities and thus that environmental security means all people have a responsibility to behave in such a way as to not impinge on the rights of others to a healthy environment. Furthermore, Barnett is adamant that a human-centered conceptualization of environmental security must not be concerned with the possibility that environmental degradation may induce violence. He argues that this is much less likely than most would suggest. Most important, however, he suggests that removing the "warfare aspect" from environmental security is crucial because it eliminates the basis on which strategic rationality gains entry into the concept. His argument is unequivocal and decidedly normative: "Because rethinking security means rethinking politics, the continued saturation of contemporary politics with issues and metaphors of violence needs to be avoided" (128).

Linking environmental security to human security involves understanding the risks to people's survival and well-being caused by environmental threats. This approach demonstrates how environmental change can have direct and immediate effects on well-being and livelihoods (Khagram, Clark, and Raad 2003: 294). But most researchers emphasize that despite the "human" in human security, understanding the relationship between environment and security demands a recognition not just of some essential "humanness" but of differences among people and the different local and global contexts in which they experience their relationship to the environment. Thus, Sanjeev Khagram, William C. Clark, and Dana Firas Raad illustrate how changes in the quality and availability of water resources can have diverse and multiple effects on the human security of different groups and individuals in a variety of different contexts. Similarly, Dalby's approach emphasizes the vulnerability of those who are most marginalized and poor globally; this kind of focus "puts human security into the circuits of the global economy" and reminds us of the connections between globalization and environmental degradation (2009: 45).

Despite this emphasis from a number of scholars on the importance of context, difference, and vulnerability, very little of the work on the environment as a human security issue foregrounds the importance of gender relations. One important exception is the work of Ursula Oswald Spring. Oswald Spring has explored the importance of gender as it relates to the human dimensions of environmental challenges. She argues that gender connects with security understood in terms of livelihood, food, health, education, public safety, and cultural diversity. In this sense, "environmental security" concerns are incorporated into human security because a healthy environment is necessary to reduce the impacts of hazards on vulnerable groups, especially women. Her latest work has been in the development of an integrated approach that sees gender, environmental, and human security as fundamentally interconnected. The idea of HUGE (human, gender, and environment) relies on a wider gender concept that includes other vulnerable groups such as children, elderly people, indigenous peoples, and minorities with a human-centered focus on environmental security challenges as well as peacebuilding and gender equity (Oswald Spring 2009: 1176). Through careful analyses of the importance of identity building and social representation—including women's socialized caring roles and the unique combination of self-sacrifice and agency involved in the ethics and practices of care as "gift-giving," Oswald Spring successfully links gender, environmental, and human security into a comprehensive and holistic vision that highlights structural insecurities and vulnerable groups.

Oswald Spring's work represents one of very few attempts to integrate gender, environmental, and human security. Theoretically, she relies on both ecofeminism and theorizations of the "gift-economy" to challenge patriarchal capitalism and Euro-American constructions of gender and the environment (1170). These themes will be addressed again later in the context of feminist environmental ethics and ecofeminism.

Ethics, Gender, and Environment

Despite the normative agenda evident in much of the environmental security literature, it remains, by and large, distinct from the literature on environmental ethics.[2] This is largely due to the central focus of most environmental ethics scholars on questions of justice and citizenship. Not surprisingly, much of this literature relies on cosmopolitan and rights-based normative frameworks; indeed, the truly planetary nature of the natural environment means that both a moral cosmopolitanism and a political cosmopolitanism are often regarded as the obvious, and perhaps the only, perspectives through which the subject can be addressed.

Rights-based approaches to environmental ethics predominate in the literature (Boyle and Anderson 1996; Hancock 2003; Hayward 2005). However, it should be noted that, within the context of environmental ethics and politics, most theorists of environmental rights emphasize the importance of correlative responsibilities. Richard Dagger, for example,

---

[2] In an overview chapter, "Green Theory," in *International Relations Theories*, Robyn Eckersley argues that green theory has a normative branch (concerned with questions of justice rights, democracy, and citizenship) and a political economy branch (concerned with understanding the relationship between the state, the economy, and the environment) (2007: 250). While this is characteristic of the tendency within this broad field to maintain sharp distinctions between different "branches," there are some authors who address the intersection between ethics, security, and political economy (see especially Dalby 2009).

argues that we must see our rights not as inviolable barriers against others but as forms of relations that entail responsibilities to others (2006: 201). Kerri Woods goes further, suggesting that human rights language could, in fact, be detrimental to the aspirations of the green movement. She points out that the state-centrism of the contemporary human rights regime is problematic in those many cases where states lack the capacity to protect the human rights of their citizens. She also argues that the "global consensus" on human rights has been and is, to varying degrees, "coerced by using human rights as a standard of civilization" (2006: 588). While these problems are not unique to environmental rights, they require special emphasis in the case of the evident "universality" and "globality" of environmental degradation.

While the cosmopolitan perspective fits comfortably with the global nature of environmental problems, theorists of environmental citizenship have moved beyond an uncritical and undifferentiated moral and political cosmopolitanism. Andrew Dobson, for example, advances a postcosmopolitan account of environmental citizenship, which relies on an "asymmetrical" account of globalization that rejects the undifferentiated "common humanity" so prevalent in much cosmopolitan literature (2003: 31). With this move, space is opened up for considering other types of moral reasoning and the virtues that accompany them, including those of care. This is not to say, however, that care figures centrally in his account of citizenship. For Dobson, care is a potential secondary virtue of citizenship that allows for the realization of the primary virtue of postcosmopolitan ecological citizenship—justice.

Also critical of the assumptions of liberal cosmopolitanism, Tim Hayward (2008) uses the case of global environmental justice to ask whether or not liberalism is capable of delivering on its universalistic moral principles. He points out that because most liberals hold the general belief that there is no tension between the political and economic aspects of liberalism, there has been virtually no recognition that the realization of universal rights—including environmental rights—may require a more "radical transformation" of global economic relations than seems to be supposed in most discussions of sustainable development. In the light of this, he argues for the need for an "ethos of restraint," and ultimately, "ecological socialism," as a means of achieving the cosmopolitan goals of universal environmental rights.

Feminist literature is the other main body of literature that diverges from liberal cosmopolitan and rights-based approaches to the environment. Like many other bodies of work addressing gender in the context of economics, politics, and society, the literature on women, gender, and the environment is formed mainly from two distinct streams: a "women and environment" stream, and an "ecofeminist" stream (Joekes et al. 1994: 137). The first, which grew out of the women in development (WID) school, emphasized women's role as environmental resource managers and their vulnerability to declines in resource availability (137). Ecofeminism, by contrast, is characterized primarily by the position that "there are important connections—historical, experiential, symbolic, theoretical—between the domination of women and the domination of nature" (Warren 1990: 126). It is often regarded as "more ideological," although, like the WID approach, it advocates "respect and support for women's efforts to conserve the environment," especially in the context of the Global or economic South (Joekes et al. 1994: 137).

Ecofeminism, in particular, has been the subject of much criticism—particularly among feminists. At its strongest, this criticism suggests that ecofeminism is fundamentally regressive and a contradictory expression of feminism (Joekes et al. 1994: 138). Specifically, Sherilyn MacGregor argues that the ecofeminist writers who celebrate women's "ethic of earthcare" fail to look behind their interpretations of women's "life-sustaining labor" to understand their "complexities, contexts and conditions" (2004: 65). Similarly, in their critique of both ecofeminism and WID approaches, Susan Joekes and colleagues argue for the need to raise questions about the broader context of patterns of resource use and resource management; in this perspective, women's (and men's) relation to environmental resources is seen as part of "general entitlements and capabilities ascribed to individuals by social relations of gender, class and so on" (1994: 139).

Both of these critiques urge a movement away from essentialisms toward an understanding of the social construction and contexts of women's relationship to the environment, as well as a recognition of the way in which gender intersects with other forms of oppression in this context. Most agree, however, on the necessity of interrogating liberalism and other dominant traditions in moral and political philosophy that ignore human embodiment and human-nature interconnections.

For example, Sherilyn MacGregor admits that the ecofeminist rejection of the independent (male) subject that obfuscates the fragility of the body, its dependence on nature or biophysical processes, and its need for care "makes sense" (2004: 60). So the question remains: Is there a way to preserve these ethical ideas while avoiding essentialisms and finding space for the politicization of women's roles vis-à-vis the environment?

Val Plumwood argues that feminist ethics may be useful to us in our understanding of the environment insofar as it discerns a false dichotomy in the choice between human and nonhuman interests and needs, as well as between care for self and care for the other, politics, and ethics. The relational concept of the self breaks down the dualism of self and other, opening ethical space for and moving emphasis to the question of how self and other are connected and can negotiate or mutually adjust; this focus, Plumwood argues, is important for addressing the environmental crisis (2006: 61). This is in line with Plumwood's idea of "hybrid ecological feminism" in which a truly human life is understood as embedded in both nature and culture. As she puts it, "Concepts of women and of the human must be rethought together in ecological terms that are respectful of non-human difference, sensitive to human continuity with non-human nature, and attentive to the embodiment of all life and the embedment of human culture in the material, ecological world" (55).

Concerns about essentialism in feminist ethics are echoed in the literature on care ethics and the environment. Here, many feminists are concerned about the tendencies toward essentialism in ecofeminism and the valorization of women's caring as "models for sustainable living"— "grassroots women" and "housewife activists" who work voluntarily to sustain life and to "fight against the powers that put that life in jeopardy" (MacGregor 2004: 57). In particular, MacGregor argues that there are political risks in celebrating women's association with caring (both as an ethic and a practice) and in reducing women's ethico-political life to care (57). Specifically, she worries that the espousal of an ethic of care has resulted in the "containment" of ecofeminist arguments: "Insofar as they attach themselves to women's specific practices and efforts to survive, they seem 'irrelevant to the moral life of the powerful'" (66).

MacGregor's prescription is evocative of the arguments made in this book. She argues that the "risks" associated with "care metaphors" would be lessened if accompanied by arguments against the exploitation of unpaid caring labor as a privatized and feminized activity and in favor of "including methods of fairly distributing necessary labour in any vision of a just and ecologically sustainable society" (69). MacGregor cites Joan Tronto's arguments in favor of a "political theory of care" in which care is seen as integral to any notion of a good society (Tronto 1993). She also cites the work of Deane Curtain, who has written about the politicization of care in the context of ecofeminist theory.

In a 1991 article, Curtain suggests that the language of rights cannot express distinctively ecofeminist insights into the treatment of nonhuman animals and the environment. Instead, he argued in favor of an alternative approach, which he calls a "politicized ecological ethic of care" (60). While Curtain raises some of the more familiar objections to a nonpoliticized ethics of care, he also puts forward a number of important insights into what a "political" ethic of care might actually mean in the context of the environment. Specifically, Curtain stresses the need to understand the ethics of care as part of a feminist political agenda: "In the mosaic of problems that constitute women's oppression in a particular context, no complete account can be given that does not make reference to the connection between women and the environment" (67). This is not to suggest that the ethics of care is a "morality for women" or that it is only of relevance to women's oppression or, in this case, to environmental issues related to women. Rather, it is to argue that making sense of the world through the lens of care ethics necessarily reveals aspects of social, political, and economic life that were previously hidden, and that significant among these are the oppression and marginalization of women. Furthermore, in this case, Curtain is suggesting that we need to understand how the effects of environmental change and degradation—such as deforestation—have a disproportionate effect on women, who are usually responsible for food preparation and the fuel and water collection required for it (66).

Curtain also rejects the idea that we can meaningfully care for distant others where there is no direct relatedness to specific others. While we may "care about," say, the plight of oppressed women in distant countries, this cannot be central to an ethics of care, since to make this move would be to lose its distinctive contextual character. He does suggest, however, that when an ethic of care is seen as part of a feminist political agenda, our instinct to "care about" may be transformed into an authentic, contextualized "caring for" when we are driven to gain an understanding of and appreciation for a particular context in which one participates (67).

While gaining this kind of understanding may be difficult and even insufficient, Curtain is certainly on to something when he suggests that an appreciation of power is what makes care ethics political and, ultimately, global. While I take issue with the idea that "caring for women . . . includes caring for their environment" (Curtain 1991: 67), I suggest that women's (and men's) ability to give and receive care is fundamentally dependent upon an understanding of our relationship to the environment and the need to treat the environment in a manner that is sustainable. A feminist ethics of care recognizes, however, that the relationship of particular persons, households, and communities to the environment is not a "natural" relationship; rather, it is one that is shaped and conditioned by politics—including the politics of gender and race, as well as wider relations of geopolitics and global political economy.

Care Ethics, Environment, and Human Security

Environmental security is a crucial aspect of human security. But "the environment" cannot simply be added to a shopping list of issues required to achieve human security. Rather, it is crucial that we conceptualize clearly our relationships to the environment and how those relationships then map on to our understandings of human security. While there is widespread anxiety about whether or not care ethics is strategically or conceptually appropriate as a lens through which to consider the relationship of human beings (and often, specifically, women) to the environment, this problem arises only when care is understood in highly essentialist, apolitical terms. However, as Curtain and MacGregor have suggested, when care ethics is politicized—through critical interrogation of the global political economy of care as part of a feminist political agenda seeking just and sustainable societies—these "dangers" are mitigated.

Considering the environment within the frame of human security reminds us that while security must confront immediate threats and vulnerabilities, it must also be attentive to long-term needs. In other words, to use the language of ecology, it must be *sustainable*. A vision of "sustainable security" has the advantage of challenging the dichotomy between the immediacy of conventional understandings of security and the "long-termism" of development approaches and of recognizing not only environmental threats but also opportunities for enhanced well-being in terms of our relationships with the environment (Khagram, Clark, and Raad 2003). A critical care ethics lens is helpful in lending ethical and theoretical weight to this idea. While the ethics of care recognizes the importance of attending to the immediate "survival" needs of particular others—for example, being able to provide clean water, adequate food, and fuel for cooking to sustain basic needs—it recognizes that care is also a long-term process. Good care requires patient attentiveness to others' needs over time; time is required in order to come to understand fully the nature and quality of others' needs and also to build opportunities for their growth and development. Thus, policies or projects geared toward sustainable security through care would consider the kinds of environmental changes that might be required to ensure that, for example, adequate firewood for cooking is available not only in the short term; it would also involve putting into place policies and programs on forestation, and the institutional and structural changes required to ensure access to these resources, in the long term. In this sense, caring for others has the immediate effect of helping to ensure the survival and security of those others and of contributing to the flourishing of those others in the long term, and of the shaping of future generations of caring citizens. Seeing human security through this lens opens up space for considering both the short- and long-term threats and opportunities present in our relationships with the environment.

A critical ethics of care creates analytical space for recognizing, and understanding, these relationships. Because it relies on a relational ontology, a critical ethics of care rejects the notion of the atomized individual as the referent of human security. Rather, the most fundamental premise of this approach is that people experience varying degrees of insecurity and security not as isolated individuals but as persons-in-relation at a variety of levels. This logic extends naturally to a consideration of our relationship to the environment. This is not to say, however, that human beings exist in relation to rocks and the sea in the same way that they exist in relation to other persons. Nor is it to say that our relations with "nature" are relations of care in the same way as our relations with other persons. An ethics of care for sustainable security is not about some kind of injunction to "care for" the environment. Indeed, there are dangers associated with paternalism that inhere in this context. On the contrary, it is about recognizing that our relationships to the environment are crucial to our ability to perform life-sustaining tasks, in both the long and the short term. A healthy biosphere is not just a background to security through care; it is inextricably intertwined with it. Soil erosion, deforestation, depletion of water reserves, climate change, and the increasing severity and frequency of "natural" disasters—all of these processes have fundamental implications for our ability to care for particular others with whom we exist in relationship. Furthermore, environmental disaster and degradation may deepen already-existing inequalities in the delivery of care and the distribution of care work; thus, certain types of environmental change may create new challenges and inequalities, especially in the way that existing gender, ethnonational, and cultural norms intersect in response to new environmental and social conditions.

A critical ethics of care recognizes that our relationships to the environment are not "natural" but fundamentally political. It starts from the position that relations of care—mediated as they are by and through relations with the environment—are important for human security insofar as they are constructed by wider contexts of global political economy, geopolitics, and cultural and ideational norms. Thus, while it is crucial to consider how our treatment of the environment will affect our long-term ability to provide care, we must also consider how these wider contexts may help, or hinder, such efforts. A critical ethics of care would reject the essentialism of some variants of ecofeminism that understand women's relationship with nature as natural; instead, the point is to understand how the association of women with nature has been used to create and sustain relations of unequal power.

Finally, because the ethics of care is explicitly a feminist theory, it recognizes the importance of unequal gendered relations of power in the context of environmental change and human security. However, as a feminist theory, it also recognizes that gender intersects with other social differences—including race, class, ethnonationality, and geopolitical location—to create relations of inequality. A feminist ethics of care in this context, however, is not geared primarily toward advancing the cause of women's equality in relation to men in terms of the natural environment—for example, in terms of access to natural resources. Rather, it is concerned with interrogating the implications of human interaction with the natural environment for assigning responsibilities for care, as well as for our ability to give and receive care adequately.

Climate Change, Care, and Human Security

While climate change is by no means the only environmental problem currently impacting human security, it is uniquely tied to a range of particular issues and threats that link closely with questions of care—including both the effect of climate change on the quality and availability of care and the distribution of care work and the relative value placed on these activities in terms of strategies for addressing climate change.

It is widely recognized that climate change has serious implications for human security. Climatic changes result in a variety of direct problems, including increased frequency of extreme weather events—such as floods, hurricanes, tsunamis, desertification, drought, and heat and cold waves. In turn, these events have important social, economic, and political effects on populations: threats to availability of food, fuel, and water, leading to serious health problems, large-scale displacement, and increased violence (WEDO 2008).

While the move to analyze the effects of climate change on human security using a "gender lens" has been slow, there is now a significant literature—from both academics and NGOs—calling for such an approach and outlining in detail the "gendered" implications of various aspects of climate change (Seager 2006; WEDO 2008). Not surprisingly, most of this literature confesses to a particular interest in the human security implications "for women," specifically; for example, the WEDO paper explains that while "this study focuses on gender equality, it emphasize the effects of climate change on women, the most disadvantaged and neglected social group in society" (2008: 1).

I question the usefulness of a gender approach in this context. While gender analysis can be instructive in revealing the social construction of "masculine" and "feminine" roles in a variety of contexts, there is a tendency—especially in NGO policy papers and briefing notes—to lapse into descriptive exercises detailing the effects of particular environmental threats on women and why these threats are more numerous, and more acute, than those facing men. There is usually a strong normative agenda lurking behind this work; however, the "gender lens" is often inadequate to analyze both the complex nature of these human security threats and the strategies available to mitigate their effects. By focusing on women, this kind of gender lens may reproduce stark dichotomies between men and women, thus obfuscating the relational nature of both men's and women's insecurity.

Jennifer Hyndman advocates going beyond gender to incorporate a fully feminist lens in order to examine how gender differences produce material, social, and other inequalities between the sexes; what other social locations produce inequalities; and how gendered identities intersect with other bases of identity and difference (2008: 103). While this approach indeed goes beyond gender to offer a more complex, critical, and potentially transformative perspective, feminism—even intersectional feminism—leaves questions concerning the ontological focus of human security unanswered. Furthermore, like a gender perspective, this kind of feminist lens runs the risk of reproducing gender dichotomies and being perceived as focusing on women's issues with respect to climate change.

A care perspective, by contrast, encompasses the critical potential of intersectional feminism while starting from the position that the need to give and receive care is shared by all people, albeit in vastly different ways depending on various contexts and relations of power. Specifically, the lens of critical care ethics reveals four crucial aspects of climate change: (1) climate change has important implications for our ability to act on our moral responsibilities, including responsibilities for care; (2) the nature and distribution of moral responsibilities arising from climate change are constructed by a series of normative and structural factors, including gender, race, and geopolitics; (3) attention to the effects of climate change on the provision and distribution of care is crucial to mitigating human insecurity related to climate change; and (4) adequate care becomes more and more difficult in the face of the effects of long-term climate change. As climate change aggravates illness and injuries caused by contaminated water, famine, and natural disasters, care work increases. Carers thus experience "time poverty," which leaves them physically and emotionally exhausted, vulnerable to infection themselves, and unable to earn an education or income (Gender Action 2009: 9).

But understanding the effects of climate change from the perspective of care does not limit the focus to traditional care work. Indeed, the provision of adequate care, and the ability to care adequately for others, requires attention to the effects of climate change on farming and food production; those responsible for farming need adaptation measures that support small-crop production and access to renewable energies inside the household for domestic use (Gender Action 2009: 8). In addition to farming, fetching water and collecting firewood—both essential for adequate care—are becoming more difficult and time-consuming tasks. Many women and girls who live in rural societies now spend up to three hours per day collecting water and firewood; as a result, their opportunities to participate in wage-earning activities are decreasing (10). Of course, it is crucial to recognize that climate change is not happening in a vacuum but rather in the context of other risks, including economic liberalization, globalization, conflict, unpredictable government policies, and risks to health, in particular HIV and AIDS, that threaten poor men and women in the Global South (Terry 2009: 6).

It is now widely accepted that climate change is increasing the intensity and magnitude of natural hazards such as floods and storms, droughts, and other severe weather events. These hazards generally have a much greater impact in income-poor countries of the Global South, where national economies lack the resources for adequate prevention, immediate relief, and rebuilding. Thus, events such as Hurricane Katrina, which hit the U.S. Gulf Coast in 2005, demonstrate starkly that even in the world's richest and most powerful country, poverty, race, and gender intersect to create an underclass who are particularly vulnerable to acute and long-term insecurity in this context (GenderCC 2009; Radford Ruether 2006).

Gender inequality related to the environment is magnified in situations of natural disasters. In general, women have reduced access to resources that are essential in disaster preparedness, mitigation, and rehabilitation. Water, sanitation, and health challenges put an extra burden on women; the already double burden of productive and reproductive labor is thus multiplied when there is a disaster and a collapse of livelihood. In many societies, sociocultural norms and caregiving responsibilities prevent women from migrating to look for shelter and work when a disaster hits (WEDO 2008). Moreover, research conducted for WHO suggests that the stress and disruption of natural disasters may lead to a rise in gender-based violence, particularly sexual violence (WHO 2008).

The UN formally recognized the importance of gender in addressing environmental disasters in the Hyogo Framework for Action, which emerged from the UN 2005 Conference on Disaster Reduction. The framework states that "a gender perspective should be integrated into all disaster risk management policies, plans and decision-making processes, including those related to risk assessment, early warning, information management, and education and training" (Enarson 2009: 4). Similarly, WHO (2009) is aware of gender differences and gender inequality relating to the effects of natural disasters. Its focus is on two areas: the increased vulnerability to sexual and domestic violence; and the extent to which women's "pre-disaster familial responsibilities are magnified and expanded by the onset of disaster or emergency, with significantly less support and resources." While both of these areas are treated with equal gravity, they are generally regarded as distinct forms of gender inequality. Furthermore, the "gender mainstreaming" perspective adopted by WHO and other UN agencies tends to focus on how gender norms lead to inequalities in the effects of disasters on men and women; while there are often token efforts to show how these inequalities affect men, usually the focus is on the effects on women. As this International Labour Organization (ILO) report demonstrates: "Men also take on new forms of work after disasters, but women's skills from their reproductive, productive and community work are especially in demand. . . . When possible, women have been found to be more proactive than men about mitigating hazardous conditions and preparing households" (Enarson 2000: 16).

My analysis does not dispute these findings but rather argues that a feminist care ethics perspective allows us to transcend these gender contests; rather than uphold this strict gender dichotomy between "men" and "women," and seek to demonstrate how women are more vulnerable and/or more proactive, an ethics of care allows us to understand how the confluence of material conditions and gender discourses leads to both increased violence and care deficits in postdisaster situations. By viewing the effects of disasters not on individuals but on individuals-in-relation, we become aware of how particular relations of dominance, or responsibilities to dependent others, are magnified or altered under disaster conditions. The discursive construction of hegemonic masculinity and "women's work" licenses men's distance from caring activities, including the activities of preservation, repair, and rebuilding in the face of massive loss. They also, in a number of contexts, license men's violence against women, especially in cases where existing protections—such as law enforcement—are absent.

The work of some feminists—while not explicitly guided by care ethics—moves in this direction. As Ursula Oswald Spring argues, strategies for addressing natural disasters must focus on innovations that can warn of impending hazards, organize evacuations, and facilitate relief and reconstruction. Planning for disasters in advance is particularly important in mitigating their harmful effects—particularly in terms of famine or violent conflict. But, she insists, to do this effectively requires an understanding of the complexity of human networks and support systems and a political commitment to aid all citizens, especially those most vulnerable to hazards (Oswald Spring 2009).

In many ways, this kind of critique and analysis is not entirely different from that surrounding the question of humanitarian intervention. A critical ethics of care focuses less on the moment of crisis than on the permanent background to any disaster situation. The relational ontology of care ethics is uniquely positioned to recognize and integrate many layers of relationships into our understanding of the environmental dimensions of human security—from the macrolevel of the relationship between human beings and the biosphere to the microlevel of household responsibilities that link care to the environment—including food preparation, water collection, household cleaning, and hygiene. As in all relations and practices related to care, gender relations and discourses of masculinity and femininity shape our understandings of the distribution of responsibilities for care and the place occupied by care in our systems of values. When we look at them through the lens of care, the environmental dimensions of human security are illuminated. This approach relies not on the "environmental rights" of all individuals but on the recognition of the crucial importance of a healthy, stable environment in ensuring that communities and families are able to give and receive adequate care.

Conclusion

Security through Care

In this book, I have illustrated the extent to which relations and practices of care are central to the struggle for basic human security. I have argued that the relational perspective of feminist care ethics can provide a critical lens through which to view human social arrangements and their effects on human security. Central to the ethics of care is the belief that relations and practices of care and responsibility are the basic substance of morality and that these relations and practices are a central feature of all human social life. The feminist orientation of care ethics, however, demands a critical interrogation of the ways in which care is socially and discursively constructed by relations and structures of gender, race, and class.

Behind every apparently autonomous individual is a constellation of care that works collectively to ensure livelihood, security, and well-being. This constellation comprises a variety of actors and institutions at many levels of personal, societal, and political life. In many instances, when we look through the lens of political and ethical liberalism, that constellation is hidden from view. For the fortunate, there is rarely even a need to consider the sources and resources of care that offer sustenance and support on a daily basis. For millions, however, inadequate or exploitative arrangements governing the giving and receiving of care threaten their basic human security on a daily basis. While this situation is most evident in developing countries of the Global South, it also occurs in many developed states, as poverty, racial and gender discrimination, and gender violence affect both local and migrant women, children, and men.

Research on care and care work over the last two decades has emphasized not only the ethics but also the politics of care. Carol Gilligan and numerous feminist moral philosophers have convincingly demonstrated how the ethics of care provides an alternative understanding of ethics that challenges conventional rights-based accounts or justice ethics. They have shown us how, rather than an "optional extra," care forms the very basis of morality upon which other moral concepts are supported. In a wonderful analogy, Annette Baier describes how rights define a sort of "individualist tip of the iceberg of morality" that is supported by the "submerged floating mass of cooperatively discharged responsibilities and socially divided labour" (1995: 25, 241). As feminists, most of these philosophers reject the separation of "ethics" and "politics" and have pointed, either implicitly or explicitly, to the political nature of care. As Joan Tronto argues, "Once we realize that moral arguments have a political context, we begin to recognize how boundaries shape morality. Widely accepted social values constitute the context within which we interpret all moral arguments" (1993: 6).

Since then, feminists have demonstrated with even greater specificity the importance of care to key institutions of politics. Selma Sevenhuijsen's groundbreaking book *Citizenship and the Ethics of Care* illustrates the necessity of locating the ethics of care within notions of citizenship, thereby opening space for carers to bring their expertise and moral considerations into public debates (1998: 15). Likewise, Carol Gould's recent book has shown how the features of care ethics— including empathetic understanding of the perspective, feelings, and needs of others—can usefully be generalized to the larger context of democratic communities (2004: 45). My 1999 book, *Globalizing Care*, explored the dominant approaches to ethics and international relations and considered the ethics of care in the context of normative IR theory. This book has built upon this work by arguing that care is central to that field of international relations normally understood as the highest of high politics: security.

Of course, advancing such an argument demands careful attention to the ways in which security is understood within international relations, as well as to the ethical basis of security. Traditional realist conceptions focus almost exclusively on the state's security in terms of military or other violent external threats posed by other actors. Usually, those other actors are external to the state and are, most commonly, other states and their militaries. While the "new security environment" of the post–Cold War world order demands attention to some nonstate actors, such as terrorist groups, the state remains the primary referent of security, and security threats are understood purely in terms of conflict or other physical violence posed by militaries or other armed groups.

Since the early 1990s, the idea of "human security" has offered an important alternative to realist understandings of national security. Based on the idea that individuals, rather than states, should constitute the primary security "referents," the human security approach reminds us that the greatest threats to security come from internal conflicts, disease, hunger, environmental contamination, or criminal violence (Newman 2010: 6–7). While many feminists have been receptive to the normative potential of the human security approach, others have questioned the implications of the ungendered "human" in human security and have called attention to particular kinds of threats facing particular humans on the basis of gender, race, and class.

I have built on this feminist critique by arguing that the individualist ontological and normative framework of conventional accounts of human security obscures from view the relations of care and responsibility required to support human life on a day-to-day basis. The struggle to ensure greater security for people must begin with attention to the state of care in their lives. Critics may argue that care is a secondary concern—that security involves addressing immediate existential threats and therefore must concentrate on military conflict and basic civil and political rights. Only once these threats are assuaged, it could be argued, do we have the luxury of considering the provision of care.

I have demonstrated, however, that care should not be considered as something only required by people who are hurt, weak, or vulnerable or who have suffered harm in some way. Rather, relations of care are the basis of all social life. In households, communities, and nation-states where the giving and receiving of care are adequate and nonexploitative, the risks associated with other kinds of security threats are reduced. Certainly, there is no single model of an adequate distribution and delivery of care; where care is chronically undervalued, however, and the services and labor of care are distributed according to particular patterns of gender, race, and class, long-term security for those people is unlikely.

Children and those who are infirm, elderly, chronically ill, or disabled all require continuous care to support their lives. Situations of violent conflict, environmental contamination or disaster, or health pandemic create a massive and immediate increase in care needs for families, communities, and, in some cases, entire nations. Providing for the needs caused by harms such as physical and psychological injury or lack of access to adequate shelter, food, and clear water depends on practices of care. The extent of these needs is exacerbated by the contemporary conditions of neoliberal globalization, which have witnessed, especially in income-poor countries of the South, a gradual erosion of state services and public support for health, education, and child care. Inequalities in the giving and receiving of care are further exacerbated by contemporary patterns of migration and trafficking of women for intimate labor; these "counter-geographies" of globalization, built on the backs of poor women of color, support the masculinized world of global finance, trade, and communications (Sassen 2002).

The politics of care and its effects on human security are clearly rooted in the material conditions of the global political economy but cannot be separated from ideological and discursive understandings of the value and role of practices of care and care work on societies. The privatization and denigration of care were crucial features of the rise of liberalism and continue to be constitutive of contemporary liberal ethics and political ideology. Liberalism's emphasis on autonomy, individual rights, and formal-legal equality depends upon the feminization and privatization of care work; as Baier explains, as long as women could be convinced to assume responsibility for the care of home and children, the liberal morality could continue to be the official morality, by turning its eyes away from the contribution made by those it excluded (1995: 25).

In many societies and at the level of global governance, liberal morality is reinforced by hegemonic masculinities that shape social arrangements, including arrangements for care. Constructions of masculinity and femininity vary according to time and place; in any given context, furthermore, multiple masculinities and femininities will almost certainly coexist. Feminists in international relations have illustrated the ways in which the rationalization of the use of force has been used to justify militarism that, in turn, normalizes and legitimates secrecy, hierarchy, hegemonic masculinism, and a culture of threat and violence (Enloe 2004: 184). However, this kind of analysis can never be reduced to the study of men and their behavior. As Enloe points out, understanding when and where masculinity is politically wielded can be understood only if one takes women's lives seriously. Women and ideas about femininity, she argues, are manipulated by political actors intent upon persuading men to behave in certain ways (184).

To understand the devaluing of care work, the lack of attention to care arrangements, the exploitation of care workers, and the neglect of those most in need of care around the world, we must pay attention to the role of constructions of masculinity and femininity in various social contexts. Hegemonic masculinities are crucial to understanding the politics of human security not just in terms of their link to militarism but also, at a deeper level, in terms of their influence over the way in which care is valued, or devalued, in societies; the normalization of existing patterns and distributions of care; and their legitimization of men's absence from caring roles. Attention to the role of hegemonic masculinities in relation to care and security forces a rethinking of dominant responses to quelling conflict and making peace.

In presenting a nonidealized conception of care ethics in the context of human security, I have sought to foreground not only its critical potential but also its possible pitfalls. When care is understood as benevolence, charity, or attention to the "victims" or the "vulnerable" in societies, an ethic of care could serve to reinforce existing patterns of domination and dependency within and among societies and at the global level. As an antidote to this, and to ensure that care ethics is clearly distinguished from the dominant "liberal internationalist" approaches to human security and global governance, I suggested the need to read care ethics through the prism of historical and contemporary relations of colonialism. This reading urges us to situate care within the frame of the colonial encounter, as well as within the context of contemporary global relations of race and geopolitics. Only then can we hope for a global commitment to care that complicates our understandings of the protectors and the protected, the strong and the vulnerable, while recognizing that shifting relations of dependence and interdependence are a normal feature of social life and global politics.

References

Agathangelou, Anna M. 2004. *The Global Political Economy of Sex: Desire, Violence and Insecurity in Mediterranean Nation-States*. New York: Palgrave Macmillan.

Agustin, Laura M. 2003. "A Migrant World of Services." *Social Politics* 10 (3): 377–396.

———. 2007. *Sex at the Margins: Migration, Labour Markets and the Rescue Industry*. London: Zed Books.

Alkire, Sabina. 2003. "A Conceptual Framework for Human Security." CRISE Working Paper 2, Centre for Research on Inequality, Human Security and Ethnicity, Oxford.

Axworthy, Lloyd. 1997. "Canada and Human Security: The Need for Leadership." *International Journal* 52:183–196.

———. 2001. "Human Security and Global Governance: Putting People First." *Global Governance* 7 (1): 19–26.

Ayoob, Mohammed. 2004. "Third World Perspectives on Humanitarian Intervention and International Administration." *Global Governance* 10 (1): 99–118.

Baier, Annette. 1995. *Moral Prejudices: Essays on Ethics*. Cambridge, MA: Harvard University Press.

Bakan, Abigail, and Daiva Stasiulus. 1997. *Not One of the Family: Foreign Domestic Workers in Canada*. Toronto: University of Toronto Press.

Barkawi, Tarak, and Mark Laffey. 2006. "The Postcolonial Moment in Security Studies." *Review of International Studies* 32 (2): 329–352.

Barnett, Jon. 2001. *The Meaning of Environmental Security: Ecological Politics and Policy in the New Security Era*. London: Zed Books.

———. 2007. "Environmental Security and Peace." *Journal of Human Security* 3 (1): 4–16.

Barnett, Michael, Hunjoon Kim, Madalene O'Donnell, and Laura Sitea. 2007. "Peacebuilding: What Is in a Name?" *International Organization* 13 (1): 35–58.

Barnett, Tony. 2006. "A Long Wave Event. HIV/AIDs, Politics, Governance and Security: Sundering the Inter-generational Bond?" *International Affairs* 82 (2): 297–313.

Baylies, Carolyn. 2000. "Perspectives on Gender and AIDS in Africa." In *AIDS, Sexuality and Gender in Africa*, ed. Carolyn Baylies and Janet Bujura, 1–24. London: Routledge.

Beauboeuf-Lafontant, Tamara. 2002. "A Womanist Experience of Caring: Understanding the Pedagogy of Exemplary Black Women Teachers." *Urban Review* 34 (1): 71–86.

Bedford, Kate. 2008. "Governing Intimacy in the World Bank." In *Global Governance: Feminist Perspectives*, ed. Shirin Rai and Georgina Waylen, 84–106. London: Palgrave.

Beneria, Lourdes. 2003. *Gender, Development and Globalization: Economics As If People Mattered*. New York: Routledge.

———. 2008. "The Crisis of Care, International Migration and Public Policy." *Feminist Economics* 14 (3): 1–21.

Ben-Porath, Sigal. 2008. "Care Ethics and Dependence—Rethinking Jus Post Bellum." *Hypatia: A Journal of Feminist Philosophy* 23 (2): 61–71.

Berman, Jacqueline. 2007. "The 'Vital Core': From Bare Life to the Biopolitics of Human Security." In *Protecting Human Security in a Post 9/11 World: Critical and Global Insights*, ed. Giorgio Shani, Makoto Sato, and Mustapha Kamal Pasha, 30–49. London: Palgrave.

Booth, Ken. 1991. "Security and Emancipation." *Review of International Studies* 17 (4): 313–327.

———. 1997. "Security and Self: Reflections of a Fallen Realist." In *Critical Security Studies: Concepts and Cases*, ed. Keith Krause and Michael C. Williams, 83–120. New York: Routledge.

———. 2007. *Theory of World Security*. Cambridge: Cambridge University Press.

Boyle, Alan, and Michael Anderson, eds. 1996. *Human Rights and Environmental Protection*. Oxford: Oxford University Press.

Bunch, Charlotte. 2004. "A Feminist Human Rights Lens." *Peace Review* 16 (1): 29–34.

Burgess, J. Peter. 2008. "The Ethical Challenges of Human Security in the Age of Globalization." In *Rethinking Human Security*, ed. Moufida Goucha and John Crowley, 49–64. Oxford: Wiley-Blackwell.

Buzan, Barry. 2004. "A Reductionist, Idealistic Notion That Adds Little Analytical Value." *Security Dialogue* 35 (3): 369–370.

c.a.s.e. collective. 2006. "Critical Approaches to Security in Europe: A Networked Manifesto." *Security Dialogue* 37 (4): 443–487.

Chandler, David, 2005. "Editor's Introduction: Peace without Politics?" *International Peacekeeping* 12 (3): 307–321.

Chang, Grace, and Kathleen Kim. 2007. "Reconceptualizing Approaches to Human Trafficking: New Directions and Perspectives from the Field(s)." *Stanford Journal of Civil Rights and Civil Liberties* 3 (2): 318–344.

Chang, Kimberly A., and L. H. M. Ling. 2000. "Globalization and Its Intimate Other: Filipina Domestic Workers in Hong Kong." In *Gender and Global Restructuring: Sightings, Sites and Resistances,* ed. Marianne H. Marchand and Anne Sisson Runyan, 30–47. London: Routledge.

Chen, L., and V. Narasimham. 2003. "Human Security and Global Health." *Journal of Human Development and Capabilities* 4 (2): 181–190.

Cockburn, Cynthia. 2004. "The Continuum of Violence: A Feminist Perspective on War and Peace." In *Sites of Violence: Gender and Conflict Zones,* ed. Wenona Mary Giles and Jennifer Hyndman, 24–44. Berkeley: University of California Press.

Cohn, Carol. 1987. "Sex and Death in the Rational World of Defense Intellectuals." *Signs* 12 (4): 687–718.

Collins, Patricia Hill. 1998. *Fighting Words: Black Women and the Search for Justice.* Minneapolis: University of Minnesota Press.

Commission on Human Security. 2003. *Human Security Now: Protecting and Empowering People.* New York: Commission on Human Security.

Connell, R. W., and James W. Messerschmidt. 2005. "Hegemonic Masculinity: Rethinking the Concept." *Gender and Society* 19 (6): 829–859.

Cooper, D. 2007. "'Well, you go there to get off': Visiting Feminist Care Ethics through a Woman's Bathhouse." *Feminist Theory* 8 (3): 243–262.

Cox, Robert, with T. Sinclair. 1996. *Approaches to World Order.* Cambridge: Cambridge University Press.

Crawford, Neta. 2002. *Argument and Change in World Politics: Ethics, Decolonization and Humanitarian Intervention.* Cambridge: Cambridge University Press.

Curtain, Dean. 1991. "Toward an Ecological Ethic of Care." *Hypatia* 6 (1): 60–74.

Dagger, Richard. 2006. "Freedom and Rights." In *Political Theory and the Ecological Challenge,* ed. Andrew Dobson and Robin Eckersley, 200–215. Cambridge: Cambridge University Press.

Dalby, Simon. 2002. *Environmental Security.* Minneapolis: University of Minnesota Press.

———. 2009. *Security and Environmental Change.* Cambridge, England: Polity Press.

Daly, Mary. 2002. "Care as a Good for Social Policy." *Journal of Social Policy* 31 (2): 251–270.

Deudney, Daniel. 2006. "Security." In *Political Theory and the Ecological Challenge,* ed. Andrew Dobson and Robin Eckersley, 232–250. Cambridge: Cambridge University Press.

De Waal, A., and A. Whiteside. 2003. "New Variant Famine: AIDS and the Food Crisis in Southern Africa." *Lancet* 362 (9391): 1234–1237.

Dobson, Andrew. 2003. *Citizenship and the Environment.* Oxford: Oxford University Press.

Duffield, Mark. 2002. "Social Reconstruction and the Radicalisation of Development: Aid as a Relation of Global Liberal Governance." *Development and Change* 33 (5): 1049–1071.

———. 2007. *Development, Security and Unending War: Governing the World of Peoples.* Cambridge, England: Polity Press.

Dunne, T., and N. Wheeler. 2004. "We the Peoples": Contending Discourses of Security in Human Rights Theory and Practice." *International Relations* 18 (1): 9–24.

Eckersley, Robyn. 2007. "Green Theory." In *International Relations Theories: Discipline and Diversity,* ed. Timothy Dunne, Milja Kurki, and Steve Smith, 247–265. Oxford: Oxford University Press.

Ehrenreich, Barbara, and Arlie Russell Hochschild. 2002. *Global Woman: Nannies, Maids and Sex Workers in the New Economy.* New York: Henry Holt.

Elbe, Stefan. 2005. "AIDS, Security, Biopolitics." *International Relations* 19 (4): 403–419.

———. 2006. "Should HIV/AIDS Be Securitized? The Ethical Dilemmas of Linking HIV/AIDS and Security." *International Studies Quarterly* 50:119–144.

Elliot, Liz. 2007. "Security, without Care: Challenges for Restorative Values in Prison." *Contemporary Justice Review* 10 (2): 193–208.

Enarson, Elaine. 2000. *Gender and Natural Disasters.* Geneva: Recover and Reconstruction Department, International Labour Office. Available at http://unisdr.org/eng/library/Literature/7566.pdf.

———. 2009. "Women, Gender and the Hyogo Platform for Action." Gender Notes No. 1. Gender and Disaster Network. Available at http://gdnonline.org/resources/GDN_gendernotes1.pdf.

Engster, Daniel. 2007. *The Heart of Justice: Care Ethics and Political Theory.* Oxford: Oxford University Press.

Enloe, Cynthia. 2004. *The Curious Feminist: Searching for Women in a New Age of Empire.* Berkeley: University of California Press.

Farer, Tom J., Daniele Archibugi, Chris Brown, Neta C. Crawford, Thomas G. Weiss, and Nicholas J. Wheeler. 2005. "Roundtable: Humanitarian Intervention after 9/11." *International Relations* 19 (2): 211–250.

Filippi, Véronique Carine Ronsmans, Oona M. R. Campbell, Wendy J. Graham, Anne Mills, Jo Borghi, Marjorie Koblinsky, and David Osrin. 2006. "Maternal Health in Poor Countries: The Broader Context and a Call for Action." *Lancet* 368 (9546): 1535–1541.

Folbre, Nancy, and Julie A. Nelson. 2000. "For Love or Money—or Both?" *Journal of Economic Perspectives* 14 (4): 123–140.

Fraser, Nancy, and Linda Gordon. 1994. "A Genealogy of Dependency: Tracing a Keyword of the U.S. Welfare State." *Signs* 19 (2): 309–336.

Frost, M. 2004. "Ethics and Global Governance: The Primacy of Constitutional Ethics." In *Global Governance in the Twenty-first Century*, ed. John N. Clarke and Geoffrey R. Edwards, 41–66. London: Palgrave Macmillan.

Fukuda-Parr, Sakido. 2004. "Gender, Globalization and New Threats to Human Security." *Peace Review* 16 (1): 35–42.

Gender Action. 2009. "Doubling the Damage: World Bank Climate Investment Funds Undermine Climate and Gender Justice." Available at http://www.gendercc.net/fileadmin/inhalte/literatur_dateien/4a03eb94920bf.pdf.

GenderCC. 2009. "Gender CC Platform for Information, Knowledge, and Networking on Gender and Climate Change." Available at http://www.gendercc.net/.

Gilligan, Carol. (1982) 1993. *In a Different Voice: Psychological Theory and Women's Development.* 2nd ed. Cambridge, MA: Harvard University Press.

Glick, P. 2003. "Parental Labour and Child Nutrition beyond Infancy." In Jody Heymann, ed., *Global Inequalities at Work*, 136–163. Oxford: Oxford University Press.

Global Coalition on Women and AIDS. 2006. *2006 Progress Report.* Geneva: UNAIDS.

Gould, Carol C. 1978. *Marx's Social Ontology: Individuality and Community in Marx's Theory of Social Reality.* Cambridge, MA: MIT Press.

———. 2004. *Globalizing Democracy and Human Rights.* Cambridge: Cambridge University Press.

Griffen, Michele. 2000. "Where Angels Fear to Tread: Trends in International Intervention." *Security Dialogue* 31:4.

Hancock, Jan. 2003. *Environmental Human Rights: Power, Ethics and Law.* Aldershot, England: Ashgate.

Hankivsky, Olena. 2004. *Social Policy and the Ethic of Care.* Vancouver: University of British Columbia Press.

———. 2006. "Imagining Ethical Globalization: The Contributions of a Care Ethic." *Journal of Global Ethics* 2 (1): 91–110.

———. Forthcoming. "The Dark Side of Care: The Push Factors of Human Trafficking." In *Feminist Ethics and Social Policy: Towards a New Global Political Economy of Care*, ed. Rianne Mahon and Fiona Robinson. Vancouver: University of British Columbia Press.

Hansen, Lene. 2000. "The Little Mermaid's Silent Security Dilemma and the Absence of Gender in the Copenhagen School." *Millennium: Journal of International Studies* 29 (2): 285–306.

———. 2006. *Security as Practice: Discourse Analysis and the Bosnian War.* London: Routledge.

Hartsock, Nancy. 1981. "Fundamental Feminism: Prospect and Perspective." In *Building Feminist Theory*, ed. Charlotte Bunch, 32–34. New York: Longman.

Hayward, Tim. 2005. *Constitutional Environmental Rights.* Oxford: Oxford University Press.

———. 2008. "International Political Theory and the Global Environment: Some Critical Questions for Liberal Cosmopolitans." *Journal of Social Philosophy* 40 (2): 276–295.

Hekman, Susan. 1995. *Moral Voices, Moral Selves: Carol Gilligan and Feminist Moral Theory.* Cambridge, England: Polity Press.

———. 1997. "Truth and Method: Feminist Standpoint Theory Revisited." *Signs: Journal of Women in Culture and Society* 22 (2): 341–363.

Held, Virginia. 1993. *Feminist Morality: Transforming Culture, Society and Politics.* Chicago: University of Chicago Press.

———. 2006. *The Ethics of Care: Personal, Political and Global.* Oxford: Oxford University Press.

Heymann, Jody. 2003a. "Introduction: The Global Spread of Risk." In *Global Inequalities at Work: Work's Impact on the Health of Individuals, Families, and Societies,* 1–12. New York: Oxford University Press.

———. 2003b. "The Impact of AIDS on Early Childhood Care and Education." UNESCO Policy Brief on Early Childhood, no. 14. Paris: UNESCO. Available at http://unesdoc.unesco.org/images/0013/001374/137400e.pdf.

Heymann, Jody, Alison Earle, and Amresh Hanchate. 2004. "Bringing a Global Perspective to Community, Work and Family: An Examination of Extended Work Hours in Families in Four Countries." *Community, Work and Family* 7 (2): 247–272.

Heymann, Jody, Alison Earle, Stephanie Simmons, Stephanie M. Breslow, and April Kuehnhoff. 2004. "The Work, Family and Equity Index: Where Does the United States Stand Globally?" Report from the Project on Global Working Families. Available at www.globalworkingfamilies.org.

Heymann, Jody, Aron Fischer, and Michal Engelman. 2003. "Labor Conditions and the Health of Children, Elderly and Disabled Family Members." In *Global Inequalities at Work: Work's Impact on the Health of Individuals, Families, and Societies,* ed. Jody Heymann, 75–104. New York: Oxford University Press.

Heyzer, Noeleen. 2006. "Combating Trafficking in Women and Children: A Gender and Human Rights Framework." In *Engendering Human Security: Feminist Perspectives,* ed. Thanh-Dam Truong, Saskia Wieringa, and Amrita Chhachhi, 110–123. London: Zed Books.

Hochschild, Arlie Russell. 2000. "Global Care Chains and Emotional Surplus Value." In *Global Capitalism,* ed. Will Hutton and Anthony Giddens, 130–146. New York: The New York Press.

Homer-Dixon, Thomas. 1999. *Environment, Scarcity and Violence.* Princeton, NJ: Princeton University Press.

Hoogensen, Gunhild, and Kristi Stuvoy. 2006. "Gender, Resistance and Human Security." *Security Dialogue* 37 (2): 207–228.

Horton, Richard. 2010. "Maternal Mortality: Surprise, Hope, and Urgent Action." *Lancet* 375 (9726): 1581–1582.

Huairou Commission. 2007. *Uniting Communities around Caregiving: Grassroots Women's Perspectives on the HIV and AIDS Pandemic.* Brooklyn, NY: Huairou Commission. Available at http://www.groots.org/download/Huairou_YWCA_Report.pdf.

Hudson, Heidi. 2005. "Doing Security As Though Humans Matter: A Feminist Perspective on Gender and the Politics of Human Security." *Security Dialogue* 36 (2): 155–174.

———. 2009. "Peacebuilding through a Gender Lens and the Challenges of Implementation in Rwanda and Côte d'Ivoire." *Security Studies* 18 (2): 287–318.

Hutchings, Kimberly. 2000. "Towards a Feminist International Ethics." Special issue, *Review of International Studies* 26:111–130.

Huysmans, Jef. 1998. "Security! What Do You Mean? From Concept to Thick Signifier." *European Journal of International Relations* 4 (2): 226–255.

———. 2006. *The Politics of Insecurity.* London: Routledge.

Hyndman, Jennifer. 2008. "Feminism, Conflict and Disasters in Post-tsunami Sri Lanka." *Gender, Technology and Development* 12 (1): 101–121.

ILO (International Labour Organization). 2004. *Global Employment Trends for Women, 2004.* Geneva: International Labour Organization.

International Commission on Intervention and State Sovereignty. 2001. *The Responsibility to Protect: Report of the International Commission on Intervention and State Sovereignty.* Ottawa: International Development Research Centre.

Jabri, Vivienne. 2007. "Solidarity and Spheres of Culture: The Cosmopolitan and the Postcolonial." *Review of International Studies* 33 (4): 715–728.

Jaeger, Hans Martin. 2007. "'Global Civil Society' and the Political Depoliticization of Global Governance." *International Political Sociology* 1 (3): 257–277.

Joekes, Susan, Noeleen Heyzer, Rith Oniang'o, and Vania Salles. 1994. "Gender, Environment and Population." *Development and Change* 25 (1): 137–165.

Kahl, Colin. 2006. *States, Security and Civil Strife in the Developing World.* Princeton, NJ: Princeton University Press.

Kaplan, Robert. 1994. "The Coming Anarchy." *Atlantic Monthly*, February. Available at http://www.theatlantic.com/magazine/archive/1994/02/the-coming-anarchy/4670/.

Kayumba, Akwilina. 2000. "The Role of Women in Taking Care of Sick Family Members in This Era of HIV/AIDS." *Journal of Social Philosophy* 31 (4): 447–452.

Kempadoo, Kamala. 2005. "From Moral Panic to Global Justice: Changing Perspectives on Trafficking." In *Trafficking and Prostitution Reconsidered: New Perspectives on Migration, Sex Work and Human Rights*, ed. Kamala Kempadoo, vii–xxxvi. Boulder, CO: Paradigm.

Kershaw, Paul, Jane Pulkingham, and Sylvia Fuller. 2008. "Expanding the Subject: Violence, Care and (In)Active Male Citizenship." *Social Politics*, 15 (2): 182–206.

Khagram, Sanjeev, William C. Clark, and Dana Firas Raad. 2003. "From the Environment and Human Security to Sustainable Security and Development." *Journal of Human Development and Capabilities* 4 (2): 289–313.

Kittay, Eva Feder. 2001. "A Feminist Public Ethic of Care Meets the New Communitarian Family Policy." *Ethics* 111 (3): 523–547.

———. 2005. "Dependency, Difference and Global Ethic of Longterm Care." *Journal of Political Philosophy* 13 (2): 443–469.

Kromhout, M. 2000. "Women and Livelihood Strategies: A Case Study of Coping with Economic Crisis through Household Management in Parmiribo, Suriname." In *Gender and Global Restructuring*, ed. M. Marchand and A. S. Runyan, 140–156. New York: Routledge.

Lawson, Victoria. 2007. "Geographies of Care and Responsibility." *Annals of the Association of American Geographers* 97 (1): 1–11.

Liden, Kristoffer. 2009. "Peace, Self-Governance and International Engagement: A Postcolonial Ethic of Liberal Peacebuilding." Paper presented at the International Studies Association conference, New York, February.

Litt, Jacquelyn S., and Mary K. Zimmerman. 2003. "Global Perspectives on Gender and Carework." *Gender and Society* 17 (2): 157.

Lu, Catherine. 2009. "Humanitarianism and the Use of Force." In *The Ethics of Global Governance*, ed. Antonio Franceschet, 85–102. Boulder, CO: Lynne Rienner.

MacGregor, Sherilyn. 2004. "From Care to Citizenship: Calling Ecofeminism Back to Politics." *Ethics and the Environment* 9 (1): 56–84.

Macklin, Audrey. 2003. "Dancing across Borders: 'Exotic Dancers,' Trafficking and Canadian Immigration Policy." *International Migration Review* 37 (2): 464–500.

Mahon, Rianne, and Fiona Robinson. Forthcoming. *Feminist Ethics and Social Policy: Towards a New Political Economy of Care*. Vancouver: University of British Columbia Press.

Marchand, M., and A. S. Runyan. 2000. "Feminist Sightings of Global Restructuring: Conceptualizations and Reconceptualizations." In *Gender and Global Restructuring: Sightings, Sights and Resistances*, 1–22. London: Routledge.

McKay, Susan, and Dyan Mazurana. 2004. *Where Are the Girls?: Girls in Fighting Forces in Northern Uganda, Sierra Leone and Mozambique: Their Lives during and after War*. Montreal: Rights and Democracy.

Mehta, Aasha Kapur, and Sreoshi Gupta. 2006. *The Impact of HIV/AIDS on Women Care Givers in Situations of Poverty: Policy Issues*. New Delhi: Indian Institute of Public Administration, Chronic Poverty Research Centre.

Miller, David. 2008. "Political Philosophy for Earthlings." In *Political Theory: Methods and Approaches*, ed. David Leopold and Marc Stears, 29–48. Oxford: Oxford University Press.

Minow, Martha. 1990. *Making All the Difference: Inclusion, Exclusion and American Law*. Ithaca, NY: Cornell University Press.

Murdoch, Iris. 1997. *Existentialists and Mystics: Writings on Philosophy and Literature*. Cambridge: Cambridge University Press.

Najafizadeh, Mehrangiz. 2003. "Women's Empowering Carework in Post-Soviet Azerbaijan." *Gender and Society* 17 (2): 293–304.

Narayan, Uma. 1995. "Colonialism and Its Others: Considerations on Rights and Care Discourses." *Hypatia* 10 (2): 133–140.

Nedelsky, Jennifer. 1993. "Reconceiving Rights as Relationship." *Review of Constitutional Studies* 1:1–26.

Nef, Jorge. 2008. "Human Security and Insecurity: A Perspective from the Other America." In *Protecting Human Security in a Post 9/11 World: Critical and Global Insights*, ed. Giorgio Shani, Makoto Sato, and Mustapha Kamal Pasha, 159–176. London: Palgrave.

Newman, Edward. 2001. "Human Security and Constructivism." *International Studies Perspectives* 2 (3): 239–251.

———. 2010. "Critical Human Security Studies." *Review of International Studies* 36 (1): 77–94.

Noddings, Nel. 1986. *Caring: A Feminine Approach to Ethics and Moral Education.* Berkeley: University of California Press.

Nuruzzaman, Mohammed. 2006. "Paradigms in Conflict: The Contested Claims of Human Security, Critical Theory and Feminism." *Cooperation and Conflict: Journal of the Nordic International Studies Association* 41 (3): 285–303.

O'Connell Davidson, Julia. 2006. "Will the Real Sex Slave Please Stand Up?" *Feminist Review* 83:4–22.

Ogata, Sadako. 2004. "The Human Security Commission's Strategy." *Peace Review* 16 (1): 2–28.

Ogden, Jessica, Simel Esim, and Caren Grown. 2006. "Expanding the Care Continuum for HIV/AIDS: Bringing Carers into Focus." *Health Policy and Planning* 21 (5): 333–342.

O'Manique, Colleen 2006. "The 'Securitisation' of HIV/AIDS in Sub-Saharan Africa: A Critical Feminist Lens." In *A Decade of Human Security: Global Governance and New Multilateralisms*, ed. Sandra J. MacLean, David R. Black, and Timothy M. Shaw, 161–178. London: Ashgate.

Orford, Anne. 2003. *Reading Humanitarian Intervention: Human Rights and the Use of Force in International Law.* Cambridge: Cambridge University Press.

Oswald Spring, Ursula. 2009. "A HUGE Gender Security Approach: Towards Human, Gender and Environmental Security." In *Facing Global Environmental Change: Environmental, Human, Energy, Food, Health and Water Security Concepts*, ed. Hans Gunter Brauch, Ursula Oswald Spring, John Grin, Czeslaw Mesjasz, Patricia Kameri-Mbote, Navnita Chadha Behera, Bechir Chourou, and Heinz Krummenacher, 1157–1181. Berlin: Springer.

Owen, Taylor. 2004. "Human Security—Conflict, Critique and Consensus: Colloquium Remarks and a Proposal for a Threshold-Based Definition." *Security Dialogue* 35 (3): 373–387.

Paris, Roland. 2001. "Human Security: Paradigm Shift or Hot Air?" *International Security* 26 (2): 87–102.

———. 2002. "International Peacebuilding and the 'Mission civilisatrice.'" *Review of International Studies* 28:635–656.

———. 2004. "Still an Inscrutable Concept." *Security Dialogue* 35 (3): 370–372.

Parreñas, Rhacel Salazar. 2001. *Servants of Globalization: Women, Migration and Domestic Work.* Stanford, CA: Stanford University Press.

Peterson, V. Spike. 2003. *A Critical Rewriting of Global Political Economy: Integrating Productive, Reproductive and Virtual Economies.* New York: Routledge.

Pettman, Jan Jindy. 1996. *Worlding Women: A Feminist International Politics.* London: Allen & Unwin.

Plumwood, Val. 2006. "Feminism." In *Political Theory and the Ecological Challenge,* ed. Andrew Dobson and Robin Eckersley, 51–74. Cambridge: Cambridge University Press.

Porter, Elisabeth. 1991. *Women and Moral Identity.* Sydney: Allen & Unwin.

———. 2006. "Can Politics Practice Compassion?" *Hypatia* 21 (4): 97–123.

———. 2007. *Peacebuilding: Women in International Perspective.* London: Routledge.

Prins, Gwyn. 2004. "AIDS and Global Security." *International Affairs* 82 (5): 931–952.

Pugh, Michael. 2005. "The Political Economy of Peacebuilding: A Critical Theory Perspective." *International Journal of Peace Studies* 10 (2): 23–42.

Quisumbing, Lourdes R. 2000. "Values Education towards a Culture of Peace." In *Male Roles, Masculinities and Violence: A Culture of Peace Perspective,* ed. Ingeborg Brienes, Robert Connell, and Ingrid Eide, 249–256. Paris: UNESCO.

Radford Ruether, Rosemary. 2005. *Integrating Ecofeminism, Globalization and World Religions.* Lanham, MA: Rowman & Littlefield.

———. 2006. "After Katrina: Poverty, Race and Environmental Degradation." *Dialog: A Journal of Theology* 45 (2): 176–183.

Raghuram, Parvati, Clare Madge, and Pat Noxolo. 2009. "Rethinking Responsibility and Care for a Postcolonial World." *Geoforum* 40:5–13.

Rai, Shirin. 2004. "Gendering Global Governance." *International Feminist Journal of Politics* 6 (4): 579–601.

Rajaraman, Divya, Alison Earle, and S. Jody Heymann. 2008. "Working HIV Care-Givers in Botswana: Spill-Over Effects on Work and Family Well-Being." *Community, Work and Family* 11 (1): 1–17.

Robinson, Fiona. 1998. "The Limits of a Rights-Based Approach to International Ethics." In *Human Rights Fifty Years On: A Reappraisal,* ed. Tony Evans, 58–76. Manchester: Manchester University Press.

———. 1999. *Globalizing Care: Ethics, Feminist Theory and International Relations.* Boulder, CO: Westview Press.

———. 2003. "NGOs and the Advancement of Economic and Social Rights: Philosophical and Practical Controversies." *International Relations* 17 (1): 79–96.

———. 2006a. "Beyond Labour Rights: The Ethics of Care and Women's Work in the Global Economy." *International Feminist Journal of Politics* 8 (3): 321–342.

———. 2006b. "Care, Gender and Global Social Justice: Rethinking Ethical Globalization." *Journal of Global Ethics* 2 (1): 5–25.

———. 2006c. "Methods of Feminist Normative Theory: A Political Ethic of Care for International Relations." In *Feminist Methodology in International Relations*, ed. Brooke Ackerly, Maria Stern, and Jacqui True, 221–240. Cambridge: Cambridge University Press.

———. 2008. "The Importance of Care in the Theory and Practice of Human Security." *Journal of International Political Theory* 4 (2): 167–188.

———. 2010. "After Liberalism in World Politics: Towards an International Political Theory of Care." *Ethics and Social Welfare* 4 (2): 130–144.

Robinson, Mary. 2005. "Human Rights, Development and Human Security." In *Human Rights in the "War on Terror,"* ed. Richard Ashby Wilson, 308–316. Cambridge: Cambridge University Press.

Ross, Heidi. 2002. "The Space between Us: The Relevance of Relational Theories to Comparative and International Education." *Comparative Education Review* 46 (4): 407–432.

Ruddick, Sara. 1980. "Maternal Thinking." *Feminist Studies* 6 (2): 342–367.

———. 1989. *Maternal Thinking: Toward a Politics of Peace.* Boston: Beacon Press.

Sarvasy, Wendy, and Patrizia Longo. 2004. "The Globalization of Care." *International Feminist Journal of Politics* 6 (3): 392–415.

Sassen, Saskia. 2002. "Women's Burden: Counter-geographies of Globalization and the Feminization of Survival." *Nordic Journal of International Law* 71:255–274.

Schellhaas C., and A. Seegers. 2009. "Peacebuilding: Imperialism's New Disguise?" *African Security Review* 18 (2): 2–15.

Seager, Joni. 2006. "Editorial: Noticing Gender (or Not) in Disasters." *Geoforum* 37:2–3.

Seeley, J., E. Kajura, C. Bachengana, M. Okongo, U. Wagner, and D. Mulder. 1993. "The Extended Family and Support for People with AIDS in a Rural Population in South West Uganda: A Safety Net with Holes?" *AIDS Care* 5 (1): 117–122.

Sevenhuijsen, Selma. 1998. *Citizenship and the Ethics of Care: Feminist Considerations of Justice, Morality and Politics.* London: Routledge.

Shani, Giorgio. 2007. "'Democratic Imperialism,' 'Neo-liberal Globalization' and Human In/Security in the Global South." In *Protecting Human Security in a Post 9/11 World: Critical and Global Insights*, ed. Giorgio Shani, Makoto Sato, and Mustapha Kamal Pasha, 17–29. London: Palgrave.

Sjoberg, Laura. 2009. "Introduction to Security Studies: Feminist Contributions." *Security Studies* 18 (2): 183–213.

Slote, Michael A. 2007. *The Ethics of Care and Empathy.* London: Routledge.

Stasiulis, Daiva, and Abigail Bakan. 2003. *Negotiating Citizenship: Migrant Women in Canada and the Global System.* Toronto: University of Toronto Press.

Steinberg, Malcolm, Saul Johnson, Gill Schierhout, and David Ndegwa. 2002. *Hitting Home: How Households Cope with the Impact of the HIV/AIDS Epidemic.*

A Survey of Households Affected by HIV/AIDS in South Africa. Washington, DC: Henry J. Kaiser Family Foundation.

Stern, Maria. 2006. "Racism, Sexism, Classism and Much More: Reading Security-Identity in Marginalized Sites." In *Feminist Methodologies for International Relations*, ed. Brooke Ackerly, Maria Stern, and Jacqui True, 174–200. Cambridge: Cambridge University Press.

Strickland, Richard. 2004. "To Have and to Hold: Women's Property and Inheritance Rights in the Context of HIV/AIDS in Sub-Saharan Africa." Working Paper, International Center for Research on Women/International Coalition on Women and AIDS, Washington, DC.

Sylvester, Christine. 2007. "Anatomy of a Footnote." *Security Dialogue* 38 (3): 547–558.

Terry, Gillian. 2009. "No Climate Justice without Gender Justice: An Overview of the Issues." *Gender and Development* 17 (1): 5–18.

Thomas, Caroline. 2000. *Global Governance, Development and Human Security: The Challenge of Poverty and Inequality*. London: Pluto Press.

———. 2001. "Global Governance, Development and Human Security: Exploring the Links." *Third World Quarterly* 22 (2): 159–175.

Thomas, Caroline, and Peter Wilkin. 1999. *Globalization, Human Security and the African Experience*. Boulder, CO: Lynne Rienner.

Thomas, Nicholas, and William T. Tow. 2002. "The Utility of Human Security: Sovereignty and Humanitarian Intervention." *Security Dialogue* 33 (2): 177–192.

Tibaijuka, A. K. 1997. "AIDS and Economic Welfare in Peasant Agriculture: Case Studies from Kagabiro Village, Kagera Region, Tanzania." *World Development* 25 (6): 963–975.

Tickner, J. Ann. 1995. "Re-visioning Security." In *International Relations Theory Today*, ed. Ken Booth and Steve Smith, 175–197. Philadelphia: Pennsylvania State University Press.

———. 2004. "Feminist Responses to International Security Studies." *Peace Review* 16 (1): 43–48.

Tiessen, Rebecca. 2006. "A Silent Killer: HIV/AIDS Metaphors and Human (In)Security in Southern Africa." In *A Decade of Human Security: Global Governance and New Multilateralisms*, ed. Sandra J. MacLean, David R. Black, and Timothy M. Shaw, 145–160. London: Ashgate.

Timothy, Kristen. 2004. "Human Security Discourse at the United Nations." *Peace Review* 16 (1): 19–24.

Tronto, Joan. 1993. *Moral Boundaries: A Political Argument for an Ethic of Care*. New York: Routledge.

———. 2008. "Is Peacekeeping Care Work? A Feminist Reflection on the 'Responsibility to Protect.'" In *Global Feminist Ethics*, ed. Rebecca Whisnant and Peggy Desautels, 179–200. Lanham, MD: Rowman & Littlefield.

———. Forthcoming. "A Democratic Feminist Ethics of Care and Global Care Workers: Citizenship and Responsibility." In *Feminist Ethics and Social Policy:*

Towards a New Global Political Economy of Care, ed. Rianne Mahon and Fiona Robinson. Vancouver: University of British Columbia Press.

Truong, Thanh-Dam. 2003. "Gender, Exploitative Migration, and the Sex Industry: A European Perspective." *Gender, Technology and Development* 7 (1): 31–52.

Truong, Thanh-Dam, Saskia Wieringa, and Emrita Chhachhi, eds. 2006. *Engendering Human Security: Feminist Perspectives*. London: Pluto Press.

Tully, James. 2002. "Political Philosophy as a Critical Activity." *Political Theory* 30 (4): 533–555.

UNAIDS. 2008. *Report on the Global AIDS Epidemic*. Geneva: Joint United Nations Programme on HIV/AIDS.

———. 2009. *AIDS Epidemic Update*. Geneva: Joint United Nations Programme on HIV/AIDS.

UNDP (United Nations Development Fund). 1994a. *Human Development Report*. New York: Oxford University Press.

———. 1994b. *New Dimensions of Human Security*. New York: Oxford University Press.

UNFPA (United Nations Population Fund). 2006a. "Factsheet 5, HIV/AIDS, Gender and Male Participation." In *Resource Pack on Gender and HIV/AIDS*. Amsterdam: UNAIDS Inter-Agency Team on Gender and HIV/AIDS. Available at http://www.unfpa.org/hiv/docs/rp/factsheets.pdf.

———. 2006b. "Factsheet 7, HIV/AIDS, Gender and Conflict Situations." In *Resource Pack on Gender and HIV/AIDS*. Amsterdam: UNAIDS Inter-Agency Team on Gender and HIV/AIDS. Available at http://www.unfpa.org/hiv/docs/rp/factsheets.pdf.

———. 2006c. "Factsheet 12: HIV/AIDS, Gender and the World of Work." In *Resource Pack on Gender and HIV/AIDS*. Amsterdam: UNAIDS Inter-Agency Team on Gender and HIV/AIDS. Available at http://www.unfpa.org/hiv/docs/rp/factsheets.pdf.

UNIFEM (United Nations Development Fund for Women). 2000. *Progress of the World's Women 2000*. New York: UNIFEM.

———. 2005. "Briefing Sheet: Migrant Women in Search of Decent Jobs." UNIFEM, September. Available at http://www.unifem.org/materials/fact_sheets.php?StoryID=302.

United Nations, International Strategy for Disaster Reduction. 2005. *Words into Action: A Guide for Implementing the Hyogo Framework*. Geneva: United Nations. Available at http://www.unisdr.org/eng/hfa/docs/Words-into-action/Words-Into-Action.pdf.

Van den Anker, Christien. 2006. "Trafficking and Women's Rights: Beyond the Sex Industry to 'Other Industries.'" *Journal of Global Ethics* 2 (2): 163–182.

Walker, Margaret Urban. 1989. "Moral Understandings: Alternative 'Epistemology' for Feminist Ethics." *Hypatia* 4 (2): 15–28.

———. 1998. *Moral Understandings: A Feminist Study in Ethics*. New York: Routledge.

————. 2003. *Moral Contexts*. Lanham, MA: Rowman & Littlefield.

Walker, R. B. J. 1992. *Inside/Outside: International Relations as Political Theory*. Cambridge: Cambridge University Press.

Warren, Karen. 1990. "The Promise and Power of Ecofeminism." *Environmental Ethics* 12 (2): 125–146.

WEDO (Women's Environment and Development Organization). 2008. *Gender, Climate Change and Human Security: Lessons from Bangladesh, Ghana and Senegal*. Available at http://www.wedo.org/wp-content/uploads/hsn-study-final-may-20-2008.pdf.

Weitzer, Ronald. 2007. "The Social Construction of Sex Trafficking: Ideology and the Institutionalization of a Moral Crusade." *Politics and Society* 35 (3): 447–475.

Whitworth, Sandra. 2004. *Men, Militarism and UN Peacekeeping: A Gendered Analysis*. Boulder, CO: Lynne Rienner.

WHO (World Health Organization). 2008. "Gender, Women and Health: Gender-Based Violence." Available at http://www.searo.who.int/en/Section13/Section390_8280.htm.

————. 2009. "Gender, Women and Health: Gender and Disaster." WHO Regional Office for South-East Asia. Available at http://www.searo.who.int/en/Section13/Section390_8282.htm.

Williams, Fiona. 2001. "In and beyond New Labour: Towards a New Political Ethics of Care." *Critical Social Policy* 21 (4): 467–493.

————. Forthcoming. "Theorizing Migration and Home-Based Care in European Welfare States." In *Feminist Ethics and Social Policy: Towards a New Political Economy of Care*, ed. Rianne Mahon and Fiona Robinson. Vancouver: University of British Columbia Press.

Williams, Michael C. 1998. "Modernity, Identity and Security: A Comment on the 'Copenhagen Controversy.'" *Review of International Studies* 23 (3): 435–440.

Will to Intervene Project. 2009. *Mobilizing the Will to Intervene: Leadership and Action to Prevent Mass Atrocities*. Montreal: Montreal Institute for Genocide and Human Rights Studies.

Woods, Kerri. 2006. "What Does the Language of Human Rights Bring to Campaigns for Environmental Justice?" *Environmental Politics* 15 (4): 572–591.

Yeates, Nicola. 2004. "Global Care Chains." *International Feminist Journal of Politics* 6 (3): 369–391.

————. 2005. "A Global Political Economy of Care." *Social Policy and Society* 4:227–234.

Young, Iris Marion. 2003. "Violence against Power: Critical Thoughts on Military Intervention." In *Ethics and Foreign Intervention*, ed. D. K. Chatterjee, and D. E. Scheid, 251–273. Cambridge: Cambridge University Press.

Zimmerman, Mary K., Jacquelyn S. Litt, and Christine E. Bose, eds. 2006. *Global Dimensions of Carework and Gender*. Stanford, CA: Stanford University Press.

Index

Aberystwyth approach to security studies, 42–43
African American women, 116–117
age-dependency ratios, 70
agency: creating/sustaining relationships, 117; of the disadvantaged, 97–99; gendered view of, 57, 94; lack of, 83; multidimensional approach to, 95; and paternalism, 108; self-sacrifice and, 83; of women, 57, 99, 108
alternative circuits of survival, 76
Annan, Kofi, 47
autonomy: distorts human picture, 90–91; enabled by women's work, 34. *See also* individual autonomy
Azerbaijan, 56, 72

beings-in-relation, 10
binary oppositions, 31–32
biosphere, 144, 155
Booth, Ken, 46
Botswana, 2, 58–59, 71
breadwinner role, 72, 74, 96

camp followers, 56
Canada: Domestic Live-In Caregiver

program, 73; female domestic workers from Philippines, 73; female share of labor force, 63, 67; health-care system, 2; human security network, 47
care economy, 124
care ethics: criticisms of, 81; dangers of idealism in, 114; environment and, 143–144, 152, 155; and exploitation, 114; and HIV/AIDS, 133–136; vs. justice ethics, 108; key attributes of, 25, 29–31; as political ethics, 90, 153; research/literature on, 24–25; transnationalization of, 134
care relations, 10; caregivers and, 135; as ethical relations, 83, 98; fundamental to human life, 90; global implications of, 112, 134; power and advantage in, 117–118; social construction of, 113–114, 128, 153
care work: cheapening of, 38; defined, 63; and girls, 70–71, 74, 129–130; in HIV/AIDS households, 129–133, 138; invisibility of, 128; lowest rung on economic ladder, 83; part of hidden economy, 124; as public value, 38; race and gender imbalance in, 115; and sexual division of

ethics, 5; and IR theory, 29; needs dialogical interplay with care, 62, 108, 119.
See also rights-based ethics
just war theory, 109

Kant, Immanuel, 112
Kantian ethics, 21
Kenya, 136
Kuwait, 67

labor: household, 132, 158; informal, 72;
invisible, 128; paid, 34, 58, 63–71;
sexual, 63, 81, 83, 164; sexual division
of, 96–97
legal reforms, 138
lens, feminist care ethics as, 51, 54–61, 80,
87, 153–160
"liberal internationalism," 105–106
liberalism: devaluing of women's work,
164; and environmental security, 149;
and good governance, 48–49, 54; liberal
peace, 111; and natural rights, 33–34;
transnational, 78
Liberia, 119
live-in caregivers, 73, 77

mail-order brides, 77
male breadwinner, 74
masculinity: dissociated from care, 35–39,
129; extreme, 80; and individualism, 22,
35; and market forces, 82; need for images of responsibility, care, 84; and rationality, 22; and responsibility to protect,
79; and violence, 35–39, 129, 136–137.
See also hegemonic masculinities
maternal health, 140
men: care work contribution of, 74; and
male irresponsibility, 37–38. *See also*
masculinity
methodology: in feminist ethics, 26–28, 44;
in human security, 15–17
migration of women, 34–35, 44–45; illegal,
57, 75; leading to lack of relationship
networks, 83–84; patterns of, 70–75;
percentage of total migrants, 64; sex
workers, 57, 75–80
militarism, 79–80

military intervention, justification for, 49,
92–95
Mohanty, Chandra, 117
monitoring and surveillance, 126
Montreal Centre for Genocide and Human
Rights Studies, 86
moral crusade against prostitution, 76
morality, 104; and environment, 152; philosophy of care ethics, 21; and relationality, 26, 29; as socially modular, 115;
universalism, 27
"moral substance," 29
mother-child model, 31
multilayered citizenship, 112

nannies, migrant, 33, 57, 64–65, 74
narrative approach to ethics, 27, 96, 102
national vs. human security, 47
natural disasters, 57–58, 155–159
naturalization of women's care work, 79, 81
naturalized epistemology, 27, 83
natural rights, 33–34
natural vs. political relationships, 155
nature and culture, 151
neocolonialism, economic and cultural, 97,
118
neoliberalism, 83; and agency, 57; effects
on Global South, 64, 164; effects on
women's care work burden, 33, 36, 83,
124, 139, 164; effect on human security,
49, 79, 102, 128; and geographies of
inequality, 84; and hegemonic masculinity, 38–39; and HIV/AIDS crisis, 128,
135; and universal human rights theory,
50
networks of care: affected by HIV/AIDS,
128–129; affected by natural disasters,
160
New Dimensions of Human Security
(UNDP), 47
new variant famine, 132
nongovernmental organizations (NGOs),
47, 72, 156
nonhuman interests, 144n1, 151–152
nonviolence in sexuality, 84
normativity, 27–28, 50, 114
Northern Ireland, 119
Norway, 47

organization of care, global, 59–60, 84
orphans: cared for by grandparents, 8, 123, 135; care needs of, 135; result of war in Azerbaijan, 56; in sub-Saharan Africa, 2, 8, 140

"Paris approach" to security studies, 42
particularism, ethics of, 30–31
paternalism: as danger to care ethics, 5, 10–11, 101, 104–106, 108, 113–121; paternalistic caring, 106, 110–112, 120–121
peacebuilding: always follows violent conflict, 107; as care practice, 108–109; language of, 104; as relationship rebuilding, 118; role of women in, 108, 119–120
Peacebuilding (Porter), 108
peacekeeping, 46, 107; as neoimperialism, 111; politics of care/compassion in, 25
permanent background of insecurity, 95, 100–102
phenomenology and ethics, 26
Philippines, 64, 68, 73
political ethics of care, 152–153
politics of conflict and peace, 107–110
Porter, Elizabeth, 24, 108
postcolonialism: responsibility and care in light of, 113–116; security studies, 43
poverty: and HIV/AIDS, 58, 124, 130–131; as security issue, 56; "time poverty," 157; from undervaluing of care work, 75; in United States, 102, 158
power: functioning through ethics, 139; makes care ethics political, 153; relations between morality and, 89–90, 118; and responsibilities, 60; underestimation of, 87
"power-over" relationships, 89
practices constitutive of morality, 25
Project on Global Working Families, 71
prostitution. *See* sex work
public-private dichotomy, 24, 31–34, 78

R2P. *See The Responsibility to Protect* (R2P)
race and ethnicity: and care work, 70, 75; intersection with gender hierarchy, 72, 91

rationality: in defining human security, 53; as masculine characteristic, 22
reflective analysis, 26
regime of labour intimacy (RLI), 78–79
relationality, 53
relational theory of care ethics, 29–30, 44–45; and environment, 154–155; and HIV/AIDS, 138–139; and human security, 54–56, 61–62
relationships of responsibility, 87–88, 133–134
relations of care. *See* care relations
relations of unequal power, 89–90
Report on the Global AIDS Epidemic (UNAIDS), 129–130
reproductive labor, purchase of, 63–64
"responsibility-for" relationships, 89
The Responsibility to Protect (R2P): as masculine image, 79, 137; seen as shift toward care ethics, 109; strengths and weaknesses of, 85–88, 93–95
rights-based ethics, 62; criticisms of, 49–50; and ecofeminism, 152; emphasis on military intervention, 95; and environment, 148–149; interpreted relationally by care ethics, 99, 113; and mass suffering, 133; as one part of solution, 62; and sex work, 77–78; state-centrism of, 149
RLI (regime of labour intimacy), 78–79
Rwanda, 101

sanitation issues, 131, 158
"secure," defined, 7
securitization, 41–42, 48, 125–127, 145
security studies, 41–46
security theory and political theory, 46
self and other, 151
self-sacrifice, 148
service dogs, 144n1
Sevenhuijsen, Selma, 28–29, 31, 162
sex, responsible, 84
sexual violence: and abortion access, 140; following disasters, 57–58, 159; vulnerability of domestic workers to, 64–65, 81; as weapon of war, 136–137, 139
sex work: and domestication of women, 81–82; exoticizing of, 82; and global

Fiona Robinson is an Associate Professor in the Department of Political Science at Carleton University. She is the author of *Globalizing Care: Ethics, Feminist Theory and International Relations* and numerous journal articles on ethics, gender, and human rights in world politics.